CASSIUS D. MCPHERSON

THOUGHTS FROM AN ADDICTED MIND

Halo ●●●●
Publishing International

ISBN: 978-1-61244-411-6
Library of Congress Control Number: 2015951481

Printed in the United States of America

Halo ● ● ● ● Published by Halo Publishing International
Publishing International 1100 NW Loop 410

Suite 700 - 176
San Antonio, Texas 78213
Toll Free 1-877-705-9647
www.halopublishing.com
e-mail: contact@halopublishing.com

To Nipu
Thanks for
your support
Cassius

First my mom Willie C Mcpherson my rock I'm missing you.
My sister Annette TB McPherson.

Always believed in me Whom I lost to the battle missing you.
The 245th cs thanks I'm proud to have served with you..

To my two mentor Melvin BoBo 3 you pushed me to
continue to learn about my roots and to thrive for the best.

Bro Christopher Blanks I thank you for your guidance
and for inviting me into your creation B.A.M.M....

Much love to all Cassius

FOREWORD

Doctors and society have labeled addiction as a plague and addicts have been cohorts to believe they are sick. So with this mentality, they enter into programs not to stop doing drugs but to be cured.

Understand that drugs of any kind are a mind altering substance. If you truly believe a program can cure you, then this needs to be repeated because you are in DENIAL, not to throw salt on recovery programs because some take this path and it works.

That's if you're trying to save your job or keep a relationship, you're going to need more than two weeks or thirty days to save your life. If you decide to change people, places and things, you will force yourself to run from humanity.

Drugs and people will always be around, it's you that has to change, not PEOPLE, not PLACES, but YOU! DRUGS make you weak; it doesn't control you. It disrupts your chain of thought. Here's what worked for me, now mind you what worked for me may not work for all addicts. So here it is...STOP!

As painful as it may be, just stop, nothing in life is easy. No, that's not true, the easiest thing we've ever done in our lives was become addicts. Don't worry about what other people think; their opinions are just that...opinions. Don't run from people, places and things, just make sound choices.

I found strength in my writings and I choose not to make many changes to the structure of this book because it's a journey. Because it shows growth. So watch as I recover through the use of mere words. Travel with me on this journey to change me...

THOUGHTS FROM AN ADDICTED MIND

CONTENTS

THOUGHTS FROM AN ADDICTED MIND

These thoughts are mixed up signals tightly jumbled in my mind.
They're trying eagerly to get out within my poetry I find.
The strength to say all the things I feel, the courage to draw the line.
These are my deepest, darkest, saddest emotions…
Thoughts from an addicted mind.

By His grace I was given this wonderful gift to use, as I deem fit.
Groups of words all jumbled inside my head; I'm trying to make sense of it.
I got down on my knees in recovery and asked Jesus to show me a sign.
He opened the gates of my imagination…
Thoughts from an addicted mind.

I flip through the pages in my mind and put together this puzzle of thoughts.
I'm beginning to reveal this person inside and the peace in which I sought.
I've gathered them all together and I can truly say there mine.
See I know from which they come from…
Thoughts from an addicted mind.

My poetry is a passion filled with paragraphs of emotion, heartache and pain.
I've unleashed these words on paper to keep me from going insane.
When I write, I'm searching my soul for something, something I can't explain.
But I'll continue to write my poetry 'cause it's giving me life again.
So here are my thoughts, in a nutshell this is the only way I could find.
To release the passion's inside of me, here are…

THOUGHTS FROM AN ADDICTED MIND

THANK YOU, LORD

GREAT IS HE

Great is He the creator, who created my family tree.
You gave your life unselfishly that day on Calvary.

Through your grace, I've opened up my heart and surrendered my will to you.
A whole New World now reveals itself and my life has become anew.

Jesus is my all and He's my beginning without an end.
It's essential I believe in Him, He died for our sins.
Great is He who comforts me; lifts me up when I feel down.
Devil be gone, my foundation is sound, my feet are on solid ground.

Through my spirit I can feel His loving touch as He fills this world with love.
Great is He who holds the key to unlock the gates of heaven above.
My heart is filled with gratitude for all that you have done.
I will serve you until you call me home; this I swear in the name of your Son.

Your power of love overwhelms me for my body is just a host.
Filled with all the greatness you put inside in the form of the Holy Ghost.
Great is He who can produce theses miracles; our lives are in His hands.
Thank you for being our guardian, through your words we understand.

A little faith is all we need to take a closer walk with thee.
Our Father laid out the plan when He first created man; you tell me…

HOW GREAT IS HE!

I KNOW JESUS LOVES ME

The weariness in my heart tries to steer me far away from you.
The deeper I reach to find your word I know this to be true.
I know Jesus loves me unconditionally 'cause He's working me every day.
He says, "Cassius, hold your head up son, this too will go away."

Now listening to an inner voice to some it may seem quite strange.
But it's the voice that's giving me the strength I need,
through Christ I've made a change.

If Jesus didn't love us, our whole world would soon collapse.
He gives us simple choices and we wind up shooting craps.
At times I feel like crying and He tells me, "Its ok."
To shed some tears is healthy if you're having a stressful day.

He caught me when I was falling; He just may have changed my fate.
If I hadn't listened when He was calling, it may have been too late.
He whispered softly in my ear, "My son, come unto me.
I'll give you everlasting life; I'll set your spirit free.
If you choose to believe I am the one and my will is all you need,
I will replace your pain with happiness. If you follow, I shall lead."

"I know you can choose between right and wrong.
I'll be right here by your side.
I know it's hard to believe and at times I grieve for your sins; this is why I died.
I gave my life so you could live and your faith is all I yearn.
And that My Father's children believe in their hearts someday I will return."

My body is just a vessel and it's holding my soul for thee.
See life is a treasure chest of dreams and it's you who holds the key.
I'm not afraid to talk to thee and I want the world to see,
A new glow now covers my outer being and I know Jesus loves me.

AGAINST ME, AGAINST GOD

When you hinder me, you strengthen me. We're two separate peas in a pod.
Your fight is not against me. Your fight is against God.
See your efforts are surly to hurt me, but I won't let you break my will.
My armor is the word of Jesus and my faith is laced with steel.
I'm in the company of angels. They go everywhere I go.
They guard me against my enemies for my Father told me so.
He will direct me to the "Y" in the road where I choose between wrong and right.
And if I stray off the righteous road, He will put you in my line of sight.

When you hinder me, you strengthen me. We're two separate peas in a pod.
Your fight is not against me. Your fight is against God.
See everything you do to weaken me makes me stronger every day.
You can continue to try to pull me down, but I will never go astray.
You can continue to try to stop me from completing His master plan.
Still I'm not going to let you sway me. My life is in His hands.

Not against me, against God and you're fighting a losing fight.
'Cause I'm wearing the full armor of God, who I pray to every night.
I'll carry His word with me every day; I'll stick to Jesus like dirt to sod.
No matter what you do against me; you are really doing against GOD.

YOUR ENEMIES HAVE A PURPOSE

Our Father has a method He uses to see if our faith is real.
He places certain people in our path just to test our will.
These people aren't really a threat to you. They're pawns like in game of chess.
And you will run into these people until the day you're laid to rest.

You may think Jesus is punishing you but that's really not the case.
See your enemies have a purpose and God's managing this race.
Struggling is not a punishment; it's part of His master plan.
To keep you strong within His word, in time you'll understand.

My enemies have a purpose. It's to keep me living straight.
Seeing past their webs of sin is something they really hate.
They can't explain this gift you have. How can you stay so strong?
It's the balance you have with Jesus that shows you right from wrong.

He's counting on you to make the right choices, but He will never leave you alone.
His shield is always covering you; to your enemies this is unknown.
But your enemies have a purpose and that purpose is to keep you strong.
If you continue to grow in the Word, you never will go wrong.

STILL STANDING

I did a nosedive on this flight called life; I mean I dove like a vulture to a feast.
Yet still humble I stand. See my life's in His hands.
On my life, Jesus holds the lease.

I've managed to punish my body, but He seems determined to keep me fit.
Every time there was a problem I didn't want to face, I'd be ready to take a hit.
I see Jesus has set forth a plan for me and His will has been oh so demanding.
I'm following His route; taking no substitutes because of Him I'm still standing.

Am I ruining the mole He made of me by indulging in manmade things?
Have I angered my savior by the choices I've made?
Will I ever receive my wings?
Many people pass judgment on my past so this pain in my chest keeps expanding.
I'm being haunted by war; all the blood and gore that I've seen.
Yet, here I'm still standing.

The hardest part of fighting this battle I'm in, is not knowing which road to take.
Still I stand at the crossroad of reality, dwelling on which choice to make.
I'm hoping the doors of life don't slam shut while
my belief in the Lord still commands me.
I have faith in my dreams, no matter how far-fetched
they seem; thank you, Jesus, I'm still standing.

MY SHIELD FROM HURT

When you cry out, "Jesus, help me!" He knows exactly what you feel.
He protects you from harm, cradles you in His arms
and surrounds you like a shield.
He'll cover you with His undying love. He'll wear you like a shirt.
But He'll never let evil to close to you. He is my shield from hurt.
Some people are put here in your life to attempt to bring you down.
It's no accident they're here in your life. Jesus wanted them around.

See they are here to try and anger you like a speed bump in the dirt.
It's really just a test to strengthen you for He is your shield from hurt.
The sooner you give in to the pain and suffering the world has put you through.
You'll see Jesus put those people in your life. He's only testing you.
You'll see the difference in your life when you learn to use the pain.
It's there to build your bond with Him then His shield you'll gain.

Always keeping Jesus abreast of things and with dangers you will flirt.
Though sometimes you may slide, Christ is right by your side.
"Here child, my shield from hurt.
My shield will cover you always even when you go astray.
Just tell me that you believe in me; I need to here you say,
'Lord, I need you in my life before they cover this vessel with dirt.'
Then you'll notice, my child,
all of the while you were covered with my shield from hurt."

THE STORM IS GOING TO BLESS ME

Everything happens for a reason and this I believe is true.
God put some people in our lives just to see what we will do.
He watches over all of us and our faith He's sure to test.
But through all adversities, He stays with you until the day you're laid to rest.
I'm confident He'll take me home and I'm sure to see,
the loved one's who have preceded me, one big happy family.

My quest is to do all the things He wants and try not to stray away.
The storm is going to bless me as long as I live His way.
I know He'll never abandon me. He'll be there in my time of need.
As long as I continue to grow in His word, my soul He will receive.
I'm convinced the storm is going to bless me for He put it here to see,
if I would grow stronger in battle with it and not let it get the best of me.

I call the storm the obstructions He uses to test our will.
They are part of a greater good you see as long as your faith is real.
Now the storm is going to bless me for as far as my eyes can see.
No burden man can bring forth in my life could take my faith from me.

CAN YOU HANDLE IT?

Life is already complicated enough without adding more stress to it.
You have to make a plan and stick to it, to your dreams you must commit.
Focus is an adversary you'll need to help you ride the storm.
Then Jesus will enter into your life in some kind of shape or form.
Like a puzzle, He'll put the pieces down and show you where they fit.
There'll be times Jesus will test your faith to see if you can handle it.

He may tempt you with drugs and alcohol; He may tempt you with money or lust.
Though temptations are strong, Jesus won't steer you wrong.
Remember IN GOD WE TRUST.
He won't pamper you like some little kid; in your hand will be your fate.
But He will catch you when you fall or when temptations become too great.
He'll never completely turn His back on you, but He'll make you want to quit.
Whatever wrong you're doing in life ask the question, "Can I handle it?"

Life is a maze of challenges woven together to keep you strong;
Giving you the peace of mind and courage to help you move along.
He'll be all the strength you'll ever need if you feel the urge to quit.
Be strong in the word of the holy one and you'll be sure to handle it.

JESUS IS MY NEW DRUG

I tried getting hi on manmade drugs and found I couldn't cope,
So I got on my knees and asked, "Please father, please release me from this dope.
It's making me lose everything I've built, got me living out on the streets,
Sleeping in boxes, abandoned buildings and using newspapers as sheets."

Unfortunately, I waited just a little too long to get back to this point,
But Jesus told me to believe and in time He will anoint.
He'll bring me, He and the father, together they'll give me a hug.
"Lay down those manmade Devil tools; allow me to be your drug.
I'll get you higher than you've ever been and you won't O.D. on me.
I won't cost a dime. You'll be high all the time. This drug I'll give you is free.
You won't have to run out and get me just call and I'll be there.
And not like the drugs you were stingy with, what I give you can share.
You can't drop me on the floor. There's no need to shake the rug.
You can halt those demons in their tracks, by saying, 'Jesus is my new drug.'"

He gets me higher than I've ever been and this high I won't have to chase.
For the more I get hi on my Jesus drug, He keeps the dope man out of my face.
He chases away my cravings and gives me room to grow.
I don't mind telling you my Jesus drug, oh yea, I need some mo'.
I admit I'm powerless over manmade drugs. I let Jesus take control.
He's all I need when those demons feed. He's the guardian of my soul.

I've given Jesus complete control. He's now the driver of this car.
He'll steer you right just pray at night. It doesn't matter who you are.
There comes a time in every life when we all may need a tug.
Let Jesus cleanse, confess your sins, let Jesus be your drug.

THE PEACE OF JESUS

I never really understood what peace was all about.
The peace of Jesus will bring you joy and make you scream and shout.
It will fill you up with joy in your time of need, shield you like a glove.
The peace of Jesus will cover you, an insurance policy from the Heavens above.
Can you imagine what peace is really like to put all your burdens in a sack?
Now throw the weight across your shoulders, let them hang down on your back.
Praise the holy name of Jesus; turn your burdens over to Him.
Watch Him take those burdens and make life look a lot less grim.
He will always be there for you no matter what you do.
He's already died for our sin's just let the healing began.
He's always there for you.
Jesus will never abandon His vessels like a captain does his ship.
Jesus understands His children and like a child we're bound to slip.
He'll never place too much in front of you but will test you every day.
And the people who are trying to hold you back, Jesus planed that way.
Those people are there to strengthen you to test your will you see.
He will place speed bumps in your life to draw you closer to thee.
So when you're feeling low and a little depressed, and want to scream and fuss.
Let go and let God give you the nod then you will feel the peace of Jesus.

I BELEIVE IN YOU

I believe all things are done for a reason and it shall come to pass.
God has a way of slowing one down when one's moving along to fast.
He will place obstacles in the road but there's one thing He won't do.
Lay to many trials and tribulations on the road in front of you.
He will test the faith you have in Him. He will let you know He cares.
He will challenge the path He's laid for you but not more than you can bear.

He giveth and He taketh away and as we live we all must die.
In life, sometimes you're happy and sometimes in life you cry.
We fear what's not there; what we can't see yet yearn what we can't touch.
Being fearful is a part of His gospel and we all should fear as much.

I fear Him for all that He has done and the things that He can do.
My fear is my faith; my fear is my strength as long as I believe in you.

WHEN HE COMES

You know He's coming back again, the only question is when.
When He comes, will you be worthy; have you confessed to Him your sins?
He suffered that day on Calvary; our burden did He bear.
I know He's coming to take me home, but will I see you there?

I'm trying to walk the righteous path the one He's laid out for me.
The Devil is trying to cover my eyes so my blessings I can't see.
He told me, "My son, stay strong in me," and gave me His holy nod.
I'm too blessed to be stressed and my mind is at rest for
I'm wearing the full armor of God.

You know He's coming back again, the only question is when.
When He gave His life upon the cross is when our lives begin.
When He comes, will you have cleansed your soul given all He has done for us?
Just as bees produce honey, the words are printed on our money,
I believe in God we trust.
For each night before I go to sleep I'm on my knees until they're numb.
I'll be there for His triumph return and ready when He comes.

I BELIEVE IN HIM

I have faith in all I have done. I believe in me you see.
All the wrong I've done is in the past and all gone because I believe in me.
I can focus on the task in front of me and not dwell on mistakes from the past.
For as long as I continue to believe in myself, I'll stay true to my life long task.
I keep crying out for stability, but my world has become a drift.
I keep praying up to my higher power to give my life a lift.
My life has become unbalanced due to some wrong turns that I made.
I started carefully pulling myself out of this hole as the darkness starts to fade.
I can't keep covering up for my past discretions by pretending they don't exist.
If I honor my Father's wishes, I'm sure to be on His home coming list.
I'll follow His words as written. In His word is where I need to be.
By walking the righteous path of my Father, in Him I believe in me.

THE LORD IN YOUR LIFE

You got to have the Lord in your life for God gave His son as a sacrifice.
He'll give you all the tools you need.
He'll give you the choices to help you remember the size of a mustard seed.
You'll benefit from your beliefs; you'll grow within His word.
There's nothing we can't ask Him for no prayer goes unheard.

Yet, why is it we only pray when things aren't going right?
See God created problems to keep us in the light.
That's why we should pray to the Father before we sleep at night.
He'll pull the wool from over your eyes, put passion in your sight.
He will place in your life obstacles to me that show's He cares.
He'll place no burden in your life He didn't think your faith could bear.

You need to have the Lord in your life and prayer is the proof you see.
He'll return your love with abundance; He's part of your family tree.
He gives all the love we need and He shares His love for free.
The Father, the Son and the Holy Ghost are all a part of the trinity.

I hope to someday find peace in life, maybe someday find a wife.
And all these things will come as long as I keep the Lord in my life.

IF ALL ELSE FAILS

When life starts crumbling around you and it takes the wind out your sails.
Get down on your knees, prayer can ease your problems if all else fails.
Life has a way of reminding you He's the guardian of the Holy Grail.
You need to get right, call on Jesus at night, He will answer if all else fails.
He'll guide you on your road to recovery. He's the hammer, you're the nails.
He'll let you choose your fate, but He will choose the date if all else fails.

Sometimes when my life is unbearable and I drop to my knees and yell.
I can't turn back to dope, in him I have hope when all else fails.
I need Jesus when sickness comes over me. He cures whatever ails.
He's all the faith I need, He removes all the greed,
He's my brother when all else fails.
My life is far from over. I flipped a coin and it landed on tails.
My foundation is set, no more Russian roulette if all else fails.
I'm praying Christ will stay by me; I was facing the gates of hell.
In His word I will stay as the pain fades away. I'll remember if all else fails.

COMPASSION, FORGIVNESS & RESPECT

He's managed to help you find yourself through times you do regret.
He's given you compassion, He's shown forgiveness and given you back respect.
Even if you step off the given path, He'll lead you back to the way.
He'll guide you back to sobriety when you fall and go astray.

Compassion is what He is showing every time you pick up again.
Forgiveness is what He is giving to you when you can't call on a friend.
Respect is what you're gaining when you build your self-esteem.
A prayer is an opened coupon on your knees you can redeem.

You know every time you pick up, you really shouldn't indulge.
You know the first hit, here you go, and from that spot you will not budge.
Your respect for life and others should not over shadow your respect for Him.
Your compassion will fade from mistakes you
made and forgiveness is looking dim.
I have compassion for recovery, forgiveness
and respect for the steps I must follow.
I must dig deep, from this disease I can't
hide and foolish pride I must swallow.

IN HIM

I've always felt His presence, but I've never seen His face.
He engulfed me with His holiness and filled me with His grace.
I talk to Him in my time of need; I know He hears my voice.
It's Him who gave me all I have, showed me I have a choice.

To live my life accordingly and try not to stray away.
I give Him all the praise's He deserves before I start my day.
I need His words to guide me for without Him I cannot cope.
I'm still alive and to my surprise, there may just be some hope.

A little faith is all you need to follow the righteous path.
On your knees say, "Please father, please," if you're faithful, do the math.
Your pains will slowly go away just ask Him when you pray.
He'll give you all the strength you need to live another day.

When we're alone we're vulnerable; our guards are lowered down.
There's strength in numbers and in recovery this is what I found.
The perseverance to move ahead is search of inner peace.
In the Lord, I found the serenity to make the cravings cease.

I believe I can make it, where at first success was slim.
Now my life's fulfilled, my destiny revealed and I found it all in Him.

ALL HE'S GOT

"Come on to me," is what He said; He'll give you all He's got.
He has a place in the kingdom, your name reserves a spot.
He listens when you pray to Him; He hears everything you say.
You have to set aside some time for Him; in His word is where I'll stay.

I can't imagine not loving Him; He never lets me down.
His blessings are abundant and He'll always be around.
Your faith is all He's asking for, a little is all you need.
Just call out His name and don't be ashamed the size of your mustard seed.
Everlasting is He's undying love; He'll give you all He's got.
We're all part of His great recovery plan, all addictions in one pot.

There's nothing you can't ask Him for, there is power in prayer you see.
As I pray for all of you, I'm asking you all to pray for me.

ASK

ASK Him to replace your unmanageability.
ASK Him to give you peace.
ASK Him to remove your shortcomings.
ASK Him to make the cravings cease.
ASK Him to give you the spiritual awaking you can't find by yourself.
ASK Him to give you serenity and to give back your health.

If you don't ask, you won't receive the blessings He has in store.
If you can't admit you're truly sick, then what are you asking for.

ASK Him for the power to maintain your sobriety when all else seems to fail.
ASK Him to take charge of your life before you wind up in jail.
ASK Him for strength to make amends to family and friends you hurt.
ASK Him for honesty to tell yourself you are addicted to chasing skirts.

Tell Him you're sorry, give life a chance, it's not an impossible task.
He listens, all you have to do is pray to Him and ASK.

GOD'S GIFT TO ME

God brought me to a place in life where I know I need to be.
My foundation is sound; from my knees I've found this was God's gift to me.

He brought me from the brinks of hell.
"Son lay your burdens down.
Your life is special; please keep my son around,
give up the booze and drugs, and I will surly set thee free.
I'll give you life as you remember just try recovery.
You need me in your corner, relax and pray to me.
You have to believe an addict alone is in bad company."

He's given me all the strength I need; His hand I gladly took.
The gift I receive from my Father didn't come from a NA book.
He rescued me from an early grave, like His son on Calvary.
He restored my faith with His love and grace; this was God's gift to me.

SERVING MY BROTHER

I can't control what others do. All I can control is me.
If serving my brother is a problem for you, this is not where you should be.
He gave us the greatest gift of all, His life for all our sins.
I couldn't do this alone and that's where He stepped in.

He took over the job of guiding me and followed as He deemed fit.
I was unsure of where I was heading. Didn't know what I was going to get.
He set the tools I needed in front of me, gave me the right to choose.
It was my decision to do what's right or refuse.

At that point, my life began to change. I had to look no further.
Now my life is complete. I never tasted defeat because I was serving my brother.

DON'T TRY THIS ALONE

Gather all the strength you have, think highly of yourself.
Confront the demons from your past; rely on no one else.
Peace will come within you; these realms are not unknown.
Look up from where you are lying down but don't try this alone.

God gave us all the right to choose; the choice is yours to make.
Success depends on the road you choose, the chances that you take.
You have the inner power; it's like using the telephone.
You have to call on somebody, just don't try it alone.

The decision you have to make is solely up to you.
Your dreams rely on the things you try, everything you do.
Your life is like a revolving door; only you can make it stop.
If you keep going around, your bottom is going to drop.

Start living in the here and now; forget the dark unknown.
It's common knowledge to live life, just don't try it alone.

YES, I CAN

Never give up on your dreams, something our Father bestowed on me.
Strive for perfection and believe in me, and I shall lay my hands on thee.
I call on my brother when I'm in doubt and He leads me by the hand.
I get down on my knees, "Please father, please," and he answers, "Yes, I can."

I'll look out for those who look out for themselves and
give praise to me when they pray.
I'm devoting my life to His word and my brother for showing me the way.
Yes, I can do anything I set my mind to do.
I can do anything if I do it in praise of you.
So guide me with your love and grace, and watch me as I grow.
I'll do what you expect of me, just to let you know.

I know you're watching over me to catch me when I fall.
You truly mean the world to me; you are my all in all.
I'm now aware of my adversities and know just where I stand.
I'm devoted to healing if GOD is willing; I believe in, "Yes, I can."

CAN YOU EXPLAIN

God will never reveal His master plan, but He will keep it simple and plain.
When He calls your name to enter where He reigns;
Will you be able to answer for the sins you did not confess?
Will you be able to lift the anvil that's resting on your chest?
Can you explain all the episodes in which you went astray?
Did you ask for His forgiveness when you got down on your knees to pray?
You know He watches while you're awake. He's your protector while you sleep.
You know it's wrong to use drugs so stick to counting sheep.

Will He recognize you as one of His own when you reach the pearly gates?
Or will He judge you like Simon on American Idol and boldly choose your fate.
You're standing in front of THE FATHER; your path has been carefully lain.
Your journey's unknown, you can tell by His tone when he asks,
"Can you explain?"

You must remember who JESUS is and how He came to be.
Without Him dying on the cross, there would be no you or me.
They say JESUS is angry when lighting strikes and He's crying when it rains.
Those tears may be for something you or I did, so I ask, "Can you explain?"
JESUS is amazing; He sees everything we do and listens to everything we say.
You can put your head under a pillow and stuff cotton in your mouth,
He still won't go away.

You know as well as I do in this life you've left a stain.
Why are you trying to cover it up when it's time will you explain?
They say an elephant never forgets and with Him it's the same.
You don't have to live a life of loneliness; this is not some kind of game.
You can try to get over JESUS; He knows all so you must be *INSANE*.
Trying to get over the creator of free will, I give up, so can you explain?

AS IF

As if I didn't see it coming. As if I already didn't know.
If I picked up and used cocaine again the road my life would go.
It lures you in like bait to a fish and before you know it you're hooked.
And before you can grasp hold to reality, your whole world has been shook.
It will rob you of your dignity and leave you a lonely shell.
As if you don't know where it's leading, it's taking you straight to hell.

As if you've never seen this life before; the Devil's got you in his grip.
Don't worry, Christ is still with you. He knows you only slipped.
I can only imagine where I would be if He hadn't taken control.
He's constantly battling the Devil's will and fighting for our souls.
He will give you the option to battle these demons
that He has allowed to cloud your view.
But He will never let you fight alone; He's always there with you.
As if you didn't know He'll be there when you call.
He'll be there like a net to a flying trapeze artist to catch you when you fall.

I can't believe I straddled the line and let SIN-sation enter my mind.
But I cried out to the Holy One; He immediately sent me a sign.
I'm ready to face reality with Him; I'll confront my fears.
I'll continue to devote my life to you; I'll never forget your tears.

As if there was ever a chance in life I could ever replace your good.
I want to thank you for all your greatness, LORD like everybody should.

DON'T GIVE IN

I'm battling these dreams I'm having of war and I'm hoping they soon will end.
I'm losing grip on reality, testing my faith, He's telling me, "Don't give in."
I'm struggling to fight off these thoughts I'm having;
they're slowly eating away at my brain.
I tried self-medication; it worsened the situation,
now I'm addicted to crack cocaine.

Now with two demons eating away at me, I ask Him, "Where do I begin?"
He says, "Start with the faith you have in me, my son, just don't give in.
See the devil will always be tempting you with me you'll have strength to prevail.
But if you let him take over your chain of thoughts,
he will drive you straight to hell.

"He's like a speed bump placed in front of you to slow life down just enough.
So he can jump in and disrupt the trinity and truly make living tuff.
But I'm here to guide you through these times and forgive you for your sins.
See I have faith in you, my son...*BELIEVE* and *DON'T GIVE IN*."

RECOVERY & STRENGTH

I AM AN ADDICT

I have admitted to the fact my life is unmanageable.
I AM AN ADDICT.
My life has caused me to do a self-evaluation of my priorities.
I AM AN ADDICT.
My war stories are reoccurring nightmares I hold close.
I AM AN ADDICT.
My recovery is mine, yet, if successful I will share.
I AM AN ADDICT.
I was selfish with my drugs, but I must be selfish with my recovery.
I AM AN ADDICT.
My foundation has levels: GOD first; KNOWLEGE second.
I AM AN ADDICT.
My ears are a sponge; my mouth is filled with cotton; each day is a struggle.
I AM AN ADDICT.
There are three words in my recovery I hold close: "IT'S YOUR CHOICE."
I AM AN ADDICT.
The motivation I put into becoming an addict, I struggle now to put into recovery.
I AM AN ADDICT.

Today and just for today, I can live with that. I am not going to dwell on the
past or worry about the future. Today I will do what I need to do to keep my
addiction in remission because if I live to see tomorrow,
I'll still be fighting pain and sorrow.
I AM AN ADDICT.

The moral of this story as I search for strength
and glory is I am doing this only for me because…
I AM AN ADDICT.

GHOST OF AN ADDICT

An empty shell of loneliness, you know you're really sick.
You see shadows in the window on the third floor those are ghosts of an addict.
Seeing images moving across the room and there's nobody there, but you.
The sounds are haunting but the drugs you're wanting and
you know not what to do.

You're seeing things that aren't really there, paranoia has taken control.
Your reality is shaken from the drugs you're taking; it's about to take its toll.
Now you can't believe it's crushing you and you're
looking all skinny and sickly.
Then you look to your left and you're all by yourself,
you scream out, "SHUT UP MICKY!"
You're walking back and forth at the window and
each time the streets are clear.
With eyes like headlights, you can't understand
why you're sweating and trembling in fear.

You're all alone, your drugs are gone, it's so quite you can't hear a peep.
Now you try to lie down after you've looked on the ground,
but the ghost won't let you sleep.
My advice to you at this point my friend is do all you can to quit.
Or be stuck in the game, he'll be there in the shadows…
THE GHOST OF AN ADDICT.

EMPTINESS

Emptiness has caused me to look deep inside my soul.
I'm trapped inside this loneliness, a dark and lonely hole.
It's one in which I dug myself and closed the door on life.
I've lost what's truly dear to me, my family and my wife.

I've rescued myself from this hell before and promised myself I'd quit.
Although I tried again, I lied and I took another hit.
Now I wallow in self-pity as I sit on this pity pot.
Yet, a small compassionate, "I got your back," would surly mean a lot.

How could I expect a helping hand from those who played a part.
The same people I reach out for help have now broken my heart.
My emptiness is self-inflicted; I choose to use again.
My emptiness is now my life line; my emptiness is my friend.

HOW CAN I?

How can I wake up every morning and face another day;
Knowing I'm the reason my life has gone astray.
How can I look in the mirror and respect the face I see;
Knowing I'm the one who caused this present misery.

How can I blame society for I'm the one who chooses this path?
Should I be ashamed when they call me names, whisper and laugh?
How could I live another day, still wishing I was high?
Should I fight the demons inside that wish I would die?

How can I not recognize my faults and face them like a man?
Grab hold to what little respect I have and come up with a master plan.
How can I ask for JESUS' help when I turned my back on him?
Should I expect him to forgive me when my world is looking grim?

How can I turn this page in life and look in the mirror at myself?
It seems I'm at this point with no options as I jeopardize my health.
How could I lose this mental stage of wishing I would die?
I'm searching for the answer, the answer to "HOW CAN I?"

ON MY KNEES

I've been in this position many times before and I wasn't looking for keys.
I was down on the floor wishing I had some more.
I was searching down on my knees.
The embarrassment never crossed my mind on how stupid I really looked.
But when I finally realized what I was doing, I knew then I was hooked.

I couldn't cry out to anyone no matter how hard I tried.
I couldn't face reality, would I become a fatality of my own selfish pride?
My hands began to look like sandpaper because I wiped them across the floor.
There was nothing there, but I didn't care, all I know is I needed more.

By this time, I knew life was unmanageable so I looked up toward the skies.
I got down on my knees, "Please take this disease, oh father, hear my cries!"
Then this calm and cool feeling came over me, my whole body felt at ease.
I put my hands together, I felt as light as a feather and for the right reasons
I was down on my knees.

FEAR & JOY CANNOT CO-EXSIST

My unconscious mind would wander, but I've never thought like this.
Throughout all this pain and suffering, fear and joy cannot co-exist.
I've tried to put these two axes together and as hard as I tried, I failed.
I'd fall flat on my face, the courts gave me a case and I watched
as my life derailed.

My fear has taken over my joy; my joy has turned into fear.
But if I had admitted I'm powerless and quitted, this road wouldn't be clear.
I'm convinced my life is unmanageable and it's obvious I couldn't cope.
I reached the end of a winding road because of my abuse of dope.

Now there are a lot of things in recovery I can add to my Don't Do list.
But one must recognize, and don't be surprised,
when fear and joy cannot co-exist.
As time passes by in your mind, you try to make the two co-exist.
But you can't mix the two and all you are going to do is put your life at risk.

Now you're deep in depression and you're asking,
"What happened to the time I missed?"
See your life is based on the choices you make
because fear and joy cannot co-exist.

I NEED YOUR SUPPORT

I'm drowning in a sea of madness and breaths are getting short.
My out stretched hands are reaching for you; I need your support.
These drugs keep calling; my self-esteem is falling, my heart begins to pound.
I'm crying out, "I need your support," as my teardrops keep falling down.

My life is cold and lonely; I keep calling out your name.
I'm fighting for my sobriety. I'm feeling so ashamed.
I'm wallowing in self-pity; I need you to be around.
I need your support to help get my feet on solid ground.
I don't need you to enable me just be there when I need.
A supportive ear to talk to when demons start to feed.

I'm trying to change my habits; I need you by my side.
Don't turn your back, don't walk away, don't runaway and hide.
I know I'm talking way too much so to make a long story short.
I need your help; I can't do this by myself…I need your support.

MADNESS TO MIRACLE

My life surrounds me with madness; it's a miracle I'm alive.
After all the drugs and booze I've done; it's a miracle I survived.
This madness has consumed me to the brink of uncertainty.
I sit back and I cry on the drugs I rely on to face my reality.

My soul is in this denial stage; I've compromised my being.
My behavior has changed, hell, I'm going insane
and an addict is what I'm seeing.
My diminishing health has me killing myself
and my principles have all but gone.
A miracle is needed to the drugs
I've conceded. I need help to carry on.

My dependency has consequently landed me in a tormented state.
I'm wandering around with my head hanging down
wondering if it's too little too late.
Now the keys to success have abandoned me;
my madness has caused me to quit.
But I can't understand why is this pipe in my hand I thought
I was through with this shit.

My drugs were playing tricks on me; out my window I started peekin'.
It was those drug filled lies and not to my surprise,
it was mostly my stinkin' thinkin'.

FAILURE IS NOT AN OPTION

My road to recovery started the day I walked into J-C.
But I didn't know my higher power had made a plan for me.
My self-esteem had been battered; my shell was frail and weak.
I had to admit to my GOD I was sick and my life was looking bleak.

I can't believe I did what I did; my life was a loaded gun.
And now my day to leave here is approaching, I want to turn and run.
I know I've built a foundation but how strong is it today.
The closer I get to leaving this place, the more I want to stay.
I'm a frail frame in a weakened state and I'm not having fun.
But I have to keep faith I'm leaving this place and failure is not an option.

I've learned some tools to guide me and my addiction is now competing.
For control of my soul, I now have a goal, in 90 days make 90 meetings.
I have to face the demons in front of me and not let them hold me back.
My addiction likes greed, it won't stop 'till I bleed,
but I'm not going to lose to crack.

My daughters support me in this fight and I have their approval nod.
I'm prepared for the fight;
I've got CHRIST in my sights and the full armor of GOD.
Fear not when your day comes to leave this place;
hold your head up and face the sun.
Have faith in yourself, say,
"I still have my health" and believe failure is not an option.

EVERYTIME I SMOKED CRACK

I envied nothing more in life then when I took a hit.
My mind was playing tricks on me; I never wanted to quit.
Deceit was strong inside of me, despair consumed my pride.
Every time I copped another bag, I would run inside and hide.

I would smoke so much my chest would hurt; it felt like a heart attack.
But would I stop, noooo! Where's the rock I dropped every time I smoked crack.

I tried to beat it on my own but the cravings made me sick.
Every time I thought I was winning, my addiction produced another trick.
I couldn't face another day. I want so bad to quit.
But before my feet could hit the ground, I was taking another hit.

I thought I could beat this I was wrong and that's a fact.
I was so conceited, my life was defeated from every time I smoked crack.

WHAT I ALWAYS DID

I am trying everything. I cannot to do what I always did.
My drugs are always haunting me. The Devil's put in his bid.
I'm bound by drugs and alcohol. I don't know what to do.
It's hard as hell to cope with this, is what I'm telling you.

I'm trying to find sobriety. I'm putting in my bid.
That's why I'm trying to do everything. I cannot do what I always did.
My life is complicated. You might not understand.
I'm trying to work this program; my life is in Jesus' hands.

What I always did was killing me. I had nowhere to turn.
A life without drugs and alcohol is truly what I yearn.
Now I'm facing a new direction and I've finally filled the slot.
But if I always do what I always did, I will always get what I always got.

CIRCLE OF HOPE

Like the rings of serenity in your life, I'll give you strength to cope.
I'll come around when you're feeling down, call on me I'm your circle of hope.
You have to believe in something. Why won't you believe in me?
I'm your circle of hope, let me cleanse you
of dope and my powers can set you free.

Don't complicate your life no more allow me to bring relief.
Don't allow booze and drugs to destroy you, I'll ease the pain and grief.
Once you commit to your circle of hope, to me, you've done your part.
Then your self-esteem will begin to gleam just let me in your heart.

I'm in you, dig deep inside yourself. I'm not that hard to find.
I'm that natural drug call dopamine resting deep inside your mind.
You must select some choices of where you want to be.
If you lift up that veil of grief, I'll surely answer thee.
I'll provide the gift of others to make your loop complete.
See the part you play in your heart I'll stay that's when your ends will meet.

Believe you can recover, release all those fears and doubts.
I'm your circle of hope, I'm stronger than dope, have faith and let me out.
I'll reveal what it means to live again. I'll grant you the tools you need.
I'll shower you with power in your darkest of hours
when those demons start to feed.

I'm your circle of hope!

DENIAL

I'm fighting the demons inside of me and it's constantly running wild.
This demon I fight so hard to defeat is the monster we call denial.
It's constantly tugging away at my soul; I'm fighting it every day.
I've admitted I'm powerless over it and it still won't go away.
It haunts me in the morning when I'm awake; it taunts me in my dreams.
Can I win the fight? I'm in day and night, it's unbearable it seems.
My denial is a demon within itself; it lives off my misery and pain.
I can't keep fighting it by myself theses cravings still remain.
Like a bad memory it's taunting me; it's always on my mind.
I hope in time I'll destroy denial that's where I'll draw the line.
I'm slowly painting a picture of what denial has done to me.
If I can replace denial with faith, my higher power will set me free.
Denial is cunning and crafty, and denial is not discrete.
Denial will crumble your will to survive or bury you six feet deep.

WHEN I PICK UP

It never really occurred to me until I heard another addict say,
I'll be hurting everyone in my family if I choose to use today.
When I pick up, my pain runs deep. My addition has a master plan.
It's out to destroy my family; the future is in my hands.
When I pick up, it's like a snowball effect; the more I use the bigger it gets.
It's a family slayer, it attacks in layers; it takes away your desire to quit.

Everyone in my family is affected by the choices I make.
The love and trust for me is affected by the chances I take.
If they support me in my recovery and each time I let them down,
What gives me the audacity to think in capacity they would stay around?
My family owes me nothing; I orchestrated this war.
When I pick up, it's me who fucked up so what am I mad at them for.

My grandkids and kids are affected when I pick up and use the pipe.
I'm in recovery today, working my problems away,
no longer will they call me hype.
If I can follow the steps in recovery, be reborn and piss clean in a cup.
I'll be able to say I am grateful today and my grandchildren I now pick up.

MY NAME IS SHAME

Like your addiction my goal is to kill you by watching you wither and wilt.
My companions are pain and depression; I'm married, my wife is guilt.
I'll do everything to divert you from your plan
and keep you chasing another hit.
That's my job, your self-esteem I'll rob 'till you just give up and quit.
I'll take away your dignity. I'll take away your pride.
And when you pick up your drug of choice…hold on, here comes the ride.

My name is Shame, you know me. I've been chilling in your brain.
'Till you use, I'll slowly pick at you then…*BAMM*…here comes the pain.
You give me so much leeway and I return your love with grief.
Then you have the nerve; what makes you think
you deserve to ask God for some relief.

You try these 12-step programs thinking they can give you peace.
My name is Shame, you know my name; on those steps I'm going to feast.
Now if you don't acknowledge my power and continue to play the game.
I'll break you down; put your ass in the ground.
You know me, my name is Shame.

I'll convince you that you can handle it 'till you're on your pity pot.
Then I'll say, "Its ok, let's make it all go away. Go ahead and smoke that rock."
If it's not clear to you, I want to kill you. That's my purpose in life you see.
Yes, my name is Shame and I thrive on your pain and with you I want to be.

LESS & NESS

There are endings in recovery we addicts know all too well.
Either they'll bring us back to reality or sink us straight to hell.
Less and Ness are common endings we often use a lot.
I put them at the end of some words and this is what I got.

I have *endless* questions to ask myself as this *emptiness* fills my soul.
It was *painless* and swift as my life went a drift.
I was lonely depressed and cold.

This *faceless* reflection revealed to me as I fell into a *bottomless* pit.
Worthless had my life become and *happiness* didn't fit.

Now *lifeless* and cold does my body feel as this *madness* consumes my being.
A *homeless useless* clump of flesh in the mirror is what I'm seeing.

Now *sadness* has engulfed me, I feel *friendless* in this fight.
The *self-centeredness* of my family has me tossing and turning at night.
Thoughtless has my family become after all the *goodness* I've done.
Senseless their actions seem; they've turned their backs to run.

But God's *greatness* has taken over me. I'm now *fearless* in this fight.
His *priceless* love now comforts me, I now choose between wrong and right.

My *carelessness* in my addiction and those *endless* roads I took.
The *togetherness* I now have with my higher power
has helped me close this book.

Now the pages are filled with *forgiveness* and the *loneliness* has gone away.
Less and Ness has more purpose now as I face another day.

FROM THE INSIDE OUT

My addiction has buried pains deep within at times I want to shout.
I need to break down these walls of misery. Be cleansed from the inside out.
My emotions are crumbling under me, can't live my life this way.
If I don't release this pressure soon my belief will go astray.

My social skills have diminished. My health has gone to shit.
But my brain has released so much dopamine that's why it's so damn hard to quit.
I want to replenish my life with joy, to ease away the pain.
I'm filled with so much remorse and anger, I'm about to go insane.

I'm trying to get my life together. I'm hoping to bridge the gap.
Yet, I can't stand the pain, am I crazy or sane with
these drugs on a plate in my lap?
My thinking is obviously eating at my will;
I can't see the forest for the trees.
I'm stuck in a rut, life is eating at my gut and
I'm doing all this using with ease.

I'm hurting all over; I'm dying inside at times I want to shout.
My life is not over and I refuse to roll-over so I'm cleansing from the inside out.

THE ILLUSION OF ACCEPTANCE

I was crazy in my addiction; I was buying all my friends.
Spending money like I was Donald Trump and living a cardinal sin.
They were grinning while in front of me, yet, laughing behind my back.
Pretending to be my friend because I was supplying all the crack.

The drug has clouded my chain of thought; I was vulnerable to them then.
Soon as the drugs got low,
their intentions would show and that's when the shit begins.
Your drugs start disappearing like magic, right before your eyes.
Cracked out to the core,
picking a lint ball up off the floor then comes the addict lies.

The illusion of acceptance was in front of me like a mystery gone astray.
Smoking drugs played a part of this madness
and my brain was like play-doh clay.
It's just an illusion you're living in, your acceptance was just a joke.
Those people gave less than a damn about you;
all they wanted to do was smoke.

Addiction is a sneaky ass predator; it's ruthless and sly as a fox.
You'll be buried alone. All your friends will be gone, just remember…
ONE BODY, ONE BOX!

BOTTOMLESS PIT

There's no end to this madness I'm in. No end within my sight.
Can't control this addiction alone, yet, I'm reaching for the light.
I'm grasping for straws in the back of my mind and each one I pull is short.
I can't understand am I less than a man for crying out for support?

The sound that echoes inside my head makes my teeth began to grit.
My hands reach to the sky while I sit there and cry.
There's no end to this bottomless pit.
I've dug this hole so deep it's like it's never going to end.
This bottomless pit is filled with shit and I don't know where it ends.

My feet keep slipping as I climb the walls in an attempt to get to the top.
If I can't stop smoking this crack cocaine, my heart is going to pop.
I need to find some solace where in society I'll fit.
I need to find a rope and put down this dope to get out of this bottomless pit.

MY ROAD

I'm looking for an exit ramp to live this life I'm in.
This road has no possibilities and crack was my best friend.

An endless, twisting, winding road, that's leading straight to hell.
If I don't get off this winding road, I'm surly bound to fail.

I'm lonely on this road I'm on; I travel by myself.
I'm speeding to an early grave. I've jeopardized my health.

My trunk is filled with baggage; this road has lots of holes.
It has no lights to follow, can't focus on my goals.

I've truly lived in darkness. It's hard to see the light.
I don't know where to turn to, I can't see wrong from right.

I'm weary in this madness, I can't do this alone.
I'm looking for some inner strength. My heart has turned to stone.

I'm standing at a crossroad, my direction is unclear.
I'm crying to the heavens, "Jesus, get me out of here!"

I've come to the conclusion that this road may have no end.
My road leads to recovery where my life will then began.

Cassius

NO GOODBYES

In life we all have ups and downs. We all have common goals.
We need to exercise our rights in order to cleanse our soul.

We have so much in common, drugs, alcohol and lies.
The same damn problem,
yet together we solved them and the demons inside have died.

With this group I've learned more about addiction and more about myself.
I can feel the pain of my addicted brothers,
through them I've gain some wealth.

As a group we battled addiction, as a group we found relief.
Though our time is short, we all shared support;
in this group I have strong belief.

Like a family we didn't always agree on things. We argued and that was it.
No punches were thrown, we all knew what to do
and the problem we had was fixed.

Our worlds where crumbling beneath our feet.
We were out there and out there bad.
But before we all leave,
we'll have time to grieve for the problems in which we had.

Behind these walls I'm safe from the world. In you does my power lie.
So I'll hold back the tears and leave without fears,
I'll be saying you no goodbyes.

Cassius

AROUND THE BLOCK

You're a lady and should always be treated as such,
but you're giving up your sweet nectar for dope.
You're the back bone of your children's lives,
without you they have no hope.

Now it's not because daddy is not around.
He's the reason you're where you're at.
He's probably the one who told you:
"Go head girl, do what you do to get what you get."

See you don't have to give up your dignity just to score a few kibbles of rock.
What you're doing is no secret, it's known all around the block.

My intentions are solely to motivate to show there is a better way.
And hopefully, my words will encourage someone to get some help today.

You don't have to be known around the block for selling your body for crack.
Your body's worth more than a hit off a pipe and a hellava lot more than a sack.

Don't play Russian roulette with your body.
There's too much evil out there to see.
Don't be out there on the streets taken a chance and wind up with HIV.

Jesus is on the other side of that door all you have to do is knock.
He will open the door and you'll be known no more
as the mouth piece around the block.

HELP

"Help me; I can't do this alone," is the hardest statement for an addict to make.
That's why we're addicts in the first place because of the choices we make.

We run and hide inside ourselves, denial is stronger than will.
You weren't worried about dying, thought our brain was frying;
it was the way drugs made you feel.

Your family watched in disbelief as you fell deeper into addiction.
You put up this front, your whole life was a stunt;
you couldn't tell what was fact or fiction.

Your body was deteriorating right before your eyes.
You got your girl heroin, your dirty draws were showing
and everything out your mouth was lies.

Not even trying to get out of this hole you dug,
you're stuck in a rut you see.
In this trap you have fallen, you hear crack
pipes a calling and you can't face reality.

You're headed for destruction, yet help is right in front of you.
The reflection you see is the portrait of me trying to tell you what to do.

Wake up and smell the coffee this vicious cycle never quits.
Ask for some help, save yourself before your bottom hits.

THE DEAD HAS ARISEN

I've been stuck in this coffin for far too long.
My addiction is like being in prison.
There's no way I can gain. Am I going insane?
Just like Christ, the dead has arisen.

Here stands before you just a shell, a vessel my soul occupies.
I can't comprehend I'm living in sin no matter how hard I try.

I'm walking a road of ungodliness. My life has hit a wall.
My way doesn't fit to His. I'll commit before my curtain call.

The stage has been set in front of me and Christ is in charge of my soul.
I can't understand; what is God's master plan?
To His will I will grasp and hold.

I've come to the conclusion inside my head I can do this and still stay straight.
I've run face first into denial; my addiction is running wild,
now my guilt has turn to hate.

I loathe the predicament I place myself in. I'm in route to a head on collision.
Now I lay here depressed, need to give life a rest for the dead has truly arisen.

EMOTIONAL

I'M STRUGGLING

I'm struggling with the fact I'm now what the government
calls collateral damage.

Just living is like having unsafe sex in fear I must now live.
Our government has truly let us down, now our children's lives we give.

America the beautiful, Home of the brave,
off our tongues these words gingerly roll.
But our children are over there dying; have you seen the latest death toll?

How deep are the cells we have to face and how far are they willing to go?
Are we willing to sacrifice our way of life or stoop to an all-time low?

Are we training them to kill us in this land of liberty?
We're spending all this money, yet some are still living in poverty.

I'm struggling to face the fact what we've done will never pass.
They're killing off our children and still making millions selling us gas.

I'm struggling 'cause Bush said the war was over. He said we had won.
Then why years later the threat is even greater and I'm in Iraq behind a gun.

I'm struggling to make ends meet, but I'm glad I didn't die.
I'm struggling for those who didn't make it. I'm struggling because of why?

I'M NOT

I'm tired of beating up on myself for the mistakes I made in the past.
The only person I really hurt is myself so the rest can kiss my ass.

I'm not going to keep saying I'm sorry for letting my family down.
I don't know if it's me or my money they miss having around.

I'm always alone in my apartment with no money or food to eat.
I've lost their respect, some support I expect;
see my family lives right up the street.

I know there's more to the problem and I'm facing that as well.
Have I caused a ripple in my family tree? Only time will tell.

I'm not going to let loneliness defeat me; I will bounce back from this.
But the love I got from my family, I do now truly miss.

I'm not going back to crack cocaine, it cost me enough you see.
I'm trying to get better as I'm writing this letter.
Have they taken their love from me?

I'll never give up on the ones I love. I'm where I want to be.
I'm not going to let my pass transgressions take my family's love from me.

EXCEPT ME AS I AM

Why must someone try to change someone there always seems to be?
A question in every relationship. "Will you change for me?"

I'm always going to be myself no matter what you do.
It always hurts the relationship when one is focused on changing you.

You can't make a zebra change its strips so why try to change my ways.
I was born this way, I have grown this way,
but I won't walk through that maze.

I've accepted the life I live today and believe I'm not promised tomorrow.
I will live with the choices I made in the past even though it causes me sorrow.

I have grieved for the life I have left behind and I pray for the days ahead,
Will be filled with the things I'm striving for 'cause my addictive past is dead.

But if you can't look past the time in my life that I didn't live as you saw fit.
You should step back and take a look at the big picture
and see the part you played in it.

I've already admitted to the wrongs I've done and for me that's good enough.
If you can't accept me as I am then you're making my love for you tuff.

I don't have to change the person I am just because you ask me to.
Then we're heading for self-destruction 'cause I'm not going
to change for you.

I'm asking you if you truly love me then except me as I am.
If you can't do this then excuse me miss 'cause I just don't give a damn.

ALL I HAVE & AM

Sometimes I feel like I'm looking at myself from the other side.
The me that I'm looking at through my tears has no morals or pride.

I see myself crying like a baby in a crib.
The only thing missing is the pamper and the bib.

The teardrops cascade down my face like the dew falls down from the trees.
It's cold and no one could tell I was crying as my tear drops start to freeze.

I can't believe I'm breaking down this is all I have and am.
But no one seems to care about me, no one gives a damn.

I don't feel sorry for myself and it's just as well for me.
I battle these demons on my own without my family.

They're fighting their own battles and frankly don't have time for mine.
I'm stronger than most of them think. I'll work this out just fine.

I've fought bigger battles then this before their support
so I just don't give a damn.
My strengths relay on me being me that's all I have and am.

TEARDROPS ARE REFLEXTIONS
FROM THE SOUL

If you could read my teardrops like the pages in a book,
You would have to dig deeper than just the surface to get a better look.

My teardrops are reflections from the soul I release to ease the pain.
From gathered up emotions kept stored within my brain.

These thoughts I keep heavily guarded way down deep inside my mind.
In a place where even the best psychologist can't unlock and find.

I store them in this hidden place to release as I deem fit.
Yet, once I let go, it becomes an overflow of emotions
that just won't seem to quit.

I carry this pain as a reminder of where I use to be.
Lately these thoughts are unbearable and are always haunting me.

I'm trying to deal with life on life's terms and deal with this arsenal of grief.
I'm fighting with forces within myself in search of some relief.

I'm running a relay race with myself and winning is my goal.
I cry to relieve my soul of life's pressures;
teardrops are reflections from the soul.

DON'T CARE IF I'M ALONE

It's easier to face my life today. I don't care if I'm alone.
This way I can conceal my feelings, the ones that are unknown.
I sit alone in my loneliness not caring who I don't see.
Sometimes in my mind, my loneliness is where I need to be.
Does this make me self-centered? Within myself am I liking this solitude?
Or am I truly mad at the rest of the world for neglecting my gratitude?
My loneliness is consuming me. I'm engulfed in this web of pain.
I'm afraid if I don't try to socialize, I'm going to go insane.
My mind is already playing tricks on me. I'm having reoccurring dreams.
I feel like I'm being pulled in both directions, slowly ripping at the seams.
But I don't care if I'm alone because it's giving me time to think.
Yet, the more time I spend in my loneliness the further I seem to sink.
It's allowing me time to gather my thoughts, my destination is still unknown.
Because I'm dealing with my loneliness all by myself, I don't care if I'm alone.

WHEN IT COMES TO PASS

I'm always looking to the skies to find my meaning in life.
An unbalanced coolness comes over me; you can cut it with a knife.
I cover my eyes to block the sun to glance up at the clouds.
I suddenly find myself saying your name silently then out loud.
These feelings coming over me is hard for me to see.
The mental and emotional pain you are causing me.
I call upon my inner strength. "How long," is what I ask.
And it answers me from inside, "You'll know when it comes to pass."
But why I'm in this state of mind, what good can come of this?
My emotions are fighting my lips I keep biting then I shiver and shake my fist.
Why am I so wrapped up in loneliness like an arm wrapped in a cast?
I need to unwind, all I need is some time; you'll know when it comes to pass.
There is this battle waged inside my head from the thoughts I have of you.
And the more the dopamine released itself, the more my passions grew.
Sometimes I want to call you just to hear your voice.
It's the chances I take, what since does
it make when I can't even make a choice.
I've grown from searching the skies for an answer and alone I'll face this task.
I'm now a man on a mission. I'm through fighting and wishing…
I'll know when it comes to pass.

ON A CLOUDY DAY

Clearly it's true my emotional stability is in question we can say.
My life is equal to a thunderstorm on a grey cloudy day.
I'm overwhelmed with problems every day to the point I hurt inside.
I try to remove these clouds from my life, disappointment is by my side.

I wish I could step outside my body and help myself cope with this.
But I can't so I'm stressed with the thought of failure
being at the top of my list.
It's embarrassing I now have to beg from others just so I can eat.
It's hard for me to except the fact I'm now facing defeat.

I have given so much to others it hurts me when I do.
I felt I shouldn't have to ask when they can see what I'm going through.
But I can't pass judgement on others 'cause they choose to treat me this way.
I'll get over this mountain I have to climb to see sunshine on a cloudy day.

SOMETIMES I WANT TO CRY

Sometimes I wonder what it was that caused me to feel this way.
I sit with my head buried deep in my hands hoping soon it will go away.

My heart beats rapidly in my chest then it's followed by an ache.
Sometimes I want to cry because the loneliness keeps me awake.

I pull the covers way up over my head to protect me from the night.
Sometimes I want to cry but instead I hold my pillow tight.

I bury my face in my pillow trying to suffocate the pain.
But no matter how hard I try, it seems to come right back again.

I try so hard not to give in, but it's eating away at my will.
A lonely shell of a man here stands, now defeated is how I feel.

The teardrops fill the wells of my eyes then roll gingerly down my face.
Though I shouldn't be crying over love, past tense, oh,
what precious time I waste.

I've rolled myself up in my emotions to my inner being it means a lot.
For my tears are very secret to me. My tears are all I got.

I cherish the solitude I have for one reason I'll tell you why.
It's all I have to hold on to that's why sometimes I want to cry.

THE OTHER SIDE OF PAIN

I can't explain this feeling, it's driving me insane.
It's hard to cope. I'm counting on hope from the other side of pain.

It's commonly known as addiction and it's freezing me like ice.
You have no clue what I'm going through and I've surly paid a price.

I've seen things I'll never forget. I've done things just as bad.
The pain runs deep, it haunts me in my sleep;
it's enough to drive a grown man mad.

I've seen bodies on the ground of Iraq I have slain.
It plays over in my brain again and again, the other side of pain.

Society calls it crazy, doctors call it post-traumatic stress.
I call it a disease that brings a man to his knees until the day he's laid to rest.

I hide so I can't be caught crying, so my teardrops mix with rain.
I have scars you can't see buried deep within me, the other side of pain.

CRANBERRY COVERED ROADS

I can't believe all the drama I've allowed to rent space in my head.
I've corrupted the lives of others and had thoughts of being dead.

I've lingered in the wrong direction to long. I believe I'm stuck in this mode.
Yet, my thoughts are uncertain. I'm in the middle of a cranberry covered road.

A winding road of pain and suffering is swimming inside my head.
I can't focus on anything inside myself and all I can see is red.

My emotions are like knots in my stomach as my memories start to erode.
I'm asking for help. I'm afraid of myself on this cranberry covered road.

I'm still fighting the craving from the drugs I took
and I'm fighting them all alone.
I'm followed around by failure, is my destiny written in stone?

I've come full circle from the addict. I was into the addict I've come to be.
I'm an addict and I'll be one 'till the day
I die and no one can take that from me.

I'm no longer trying to be slick and devious.
My addiction is like breaking a code.
But, I won't let this sway me from the path
I've choose on this cranberry covered road.

I WONDER IF DYING IS SO BAD

My life has hit rock bottom. I wonder if I should go.
My family has disowned me and my self-esteem is low.

I looked at where I was; now I look at where I'm at.
I have no one to turn to and nowhere to lay my hat.

I feel like I've failed everyone, especially myself.
No one comes by or calls me and I don't know anyone else.

All my so-called friends are probably laughing behind my back.
But they were all my buddies when I was supplying the booze or sack.

Now I sit alone in the hospital, my future is unclear.
Deep in my mind I'm telling myself, "I don't want to be here."

I wonder if dying is so bad. At lease I'll have peace of mind.
Being here is only helping me and the people here are kind.

My health was slowly deteriorating. They're trying to get me right.
When I sleep, I toss and turn and dream. I'm up most of the night.

I'm trying to get back where I was. My future is looking bleak.
I'm searching for my inner strength to find the life I seek.

Love has bounced my life around. I guess that's why I'm mad.
I guess that's why I keep asking myself, "I wonder if dying is so bad?"

I'm writing this to vent my thoughts. I'd never take my life.
God is my armor and shield to ease life's tolls and strife.

PICTURES FROM MY PAST

Like a slideshow in the back of my mind, like a shadow when it is cast.
The darkness has engulfed my soul, pictures from the past.
Sitting on my living room couch with a crack pipe in my hand,
Seems my family has turned its back on me. They just don't understand.
What I have is a disease not a problem like they think.
They turned their backs on a wounded ship now they watch me as I sink.
This pain is really hurting me, addiction has kicked my ass.
It's waiting here for me to slip pictures in from my past.
I can't imagine where I'd be if I didn't come to this place.
I now believe that commercial, the mind is a terrible thing to waste.
Yet, here I sit hurting to use again, don't know how long this will last.
I can't get these images from my mind, pictures from the past.

ME, MYSELF & I

"I'm never really lonely," that's what I use to say.
But I'd often ask my higher power, "Why do I feel this way?"

I'd ask before I'd go to bed and lay me down to sleep.
Sometimes in my addiction I would huddle in the corner like a child and weep.

I felt I had nobody. I'd fall to my knees and cry.
In reality, I was never alone. I had Me, Myself and I.

Me was my inner strength I called on when I was mad.
Myself was my comforter I needed when I was sad.

I was always with Me to guide me through the night.
But, where was I the night I let my addiction cloud my site.

I haven't been doing this all my life. How did I get hooked so fast?
I have to let go and let God in 'cause life is kicking my ass.

How could I let Myself disrupt my life with years of drinking, but I'm not sick.
If I wouldn't allow Myself to buy the drugs this damn addiction I could kick.

Me, Myself and I, can't do it. I need to set two free.
Now my road is clear, no more drugs or fear. It's just Me…
and SOBRIETY.

LOVING YOU

I TOUCHED A DREAM

Mere words cannot explain the way you truly make me feel.
I find it hard to breath in your presence. I know this must be real.
I reach out my hand to hold you; *your skin feels like a dove.*
I cried out to the heavens for God to bless me, please let this be love.
My searching seemed forever, yes, forever so it seems.
I thought to myself, *Is it possible, could one truly touch a dream?*

I never felt this way before and yet it feel so real.
Your love is magical to me. It gives me such a thrill.
If loving you is meant to be then teach me what to do.
'Cause I don't plan on making the fatal mistake that leads to losing you.

I may be loving you too much, to the point of no return.
My heart and soul is on fire for you. Your love is what I yearn.
When I close my eyes at night to sleep, my thoughts are of only you.
And the more I see you in my mind the more my passions grew.

It's common, don't you understand, I need you by my side.
If you're not feeling what I feel then again my heart has lied.
I need you like toast needs butter. You're the coffee and I'm the cream.
I knew from the start down deep in my heart that I have truly touched a dream.

I CAN'T GET OVER YOU

I've relinquish myself of everything that reminds me of you.
I've ridded myself of the memories although all I have are few.
Still the ones I have stay with me and no matter what I do.
I find myself overwhelmed with thoughts I can't get over you.

My dreams are a constant picture book; on every page I see your face.
In my heart, I've built a monument in which you hold a special space.
I promised myself I wouldn't hurt that I wouldn't shed a tear.
Still I'm dying inside, though the tears have dried, the fact is I want you here.

I sit silently waiting for you to call, but I know this won't come true.
In my dreams, I'm holding you close to me because I can't get over you.
My body cringes from the mere thought of someone holding you at night.
But I calm myself when I'm sleeping, by simply holding my pillow tight.

I have to be strong, was what we were doing
so wrong 'cause I can't get over you.

LAST NIGHT I CRIED

Last night I cried emotionally,
physically releasing a pool of pain that had me trapped.
Trapped inside a circle of madness revolving around this core of happiness
caused by feelings of passion that unleashed this fire, a fire inside what was
once a cold shell of a man.

Last night I cried. I cried a pool of tears fueled with enough rage to cause a
nuclear explosion by a heart damaged by the unloved. Fixated on not allowing
myself to feel, my will has been damaged, neglected, disrespected,
I challenge myself to love.

Last night I cried again…and again…and again…
stuck in this mode. What can I do?
My life has become a clash of sections, involuntary erections, yet, in all
directions I turn to face the reality last night I cried. I cried last night.

Last night I cleansed my soul with tears. I cried 'till the wells of my eyes dried
and as I wiped the tears from my face, I realized my tears were merely episodes
of the past hurts dying to be released so I released them last night.
Last night I cried.

BROWN EYED GIRL

I imagine what the world would see if it saw things through your eyes.
Your beauty would engulf the world with peace
and truth would prevail from lies.
Harmony would overcome violence, peace would rise like stock.
There would be no more war just what I'm hoping for in Afghanistan and Iraq.

Mere words can't express the stories I see down deep within your glow.
Your lovely eyes have stories I think the world needs to know.
Stories that have touched my soul in ways I never knew.
I thank the Lord for guiding me to the path of meeting you.

You've bestowed on to me the will to live. You turn darkness into light.
I wish I could hold you if only for one night.
My life was filled with sadness, but you made me want to sing.
Even though I just met you brown eyed girl,
you're the wind beneath my wings.

Though I really don't know you, in my sight you are a pearl.
You are the best thing that never happened to me,
my imaginary brown eyed girl.

FAR AWAY

Longing for an everlasting love, yet you're so far away.
I crave to hold you in my arms and make you want to stay.
I dream of holding you every night. In my mind I want to scream.
But then I realize in my mind, I only touched a dream.

I shiver every time you speak as I gaze into your eyes.
Will you ever love me like I love you, please cupid here my cries.
You have to understand my love to you I want to give.
My world, my all, my everything, you are my will to live.

I think about you all the time. You're always on my mind.
It's you I prayed to the heavens for when I asked Him for a sign.
You gracefully walked into my life and made my life worth living.
Yet, far away all I can say, you're worth the love I'm giving.

Say you'll stay forever mine and our love is really true.
Because I'm holding on to happiness when I'm holding on to you.
You give my world a different meaning when I glance upon your face.
Each moment I share with you, not a second would I waste.

So given all I've said in these words, I promise you this today,
I'll love you 'till the day I die though your love is far away.

WHY

In my mind, I have this question and no matter how hard I try...
It keeps coming back to taunt me. The question I have is, "Why?"
Why did you ever touch me, allow me to get so close to you.
My heart is broken, this ain't no joke and now I wonder who.

Who has stepped into the space I had and taken up my place.
I can't control my emotions every time I see your face.
I'm trying hard to get over you. It's hard to let you go.
Girl, can't you see what you're doing to me? My self-esteem is low.

How could you hurt somebody who gave you all he had?
I don't deserve this heartache. Was loving me so bad?
I allowed this love to happen though I knew it wouldn't last.
My track record often speaks for itself. I fall in love too fast.

I can't control these feelings, my emotions are running wild.
Although I know you won't answer when I call, I still pick up and dial.
I need to hear your voice, and then I break down and cry.
Can you do a broken man a favor and answer the question, "WHY?"

WHY DO I FEEL THIS WAY?

I can't explain this loneliness or why it's eating away inside.
There are days I just want to give up living, just runaway and hide.
My dreams have become nightmares. My nightmares interrupt my sleep.
Then I find myself curled up like a baby as I lie awake and weep.

My thoughts have fallen on deaf ears. It's hard for me to cope.
If I can't erase these memories, I'll have to rely on hope.
To comfort me in my time of need to keep me from going insane.
Oh Jesus, why do I feel this way? Why is there so much pain?

My dreams have taken over reality and I can't control my thoughts.
I guess that's why I'm so empty inside. I've lost the love I sought.
Now every time I try to get close to someone
there's this burning inside my chest.
I want to give in then they say let's be friends,
again my heart has been laid to rest.

I'm so angry because I can't find true love or true love just won't find me.
I guess I'm destined to be by myself that's the way it's supposed to be.
I try hard to cope with the way I feel but it haunts me every day.
I guess there's no hope, I'm not meant to cope with…
Why do I feel this way?

I CAN'T THINK STRAIGHT

From the very first time I saw your face, I knew it had to be fate.
I had to ask myself over and over, why I can't think straight.
Every thought I had in my head were only my thoughts of you.
I can't think straight but it sure felt great, I knew not what to do.

I'm challenging myself in life to find a love that's right.
But givin' my track record in relationships, I can't take loving lite.
I'm trying not to fall apart but no matter how hard I try.
I slip right back into depression and all I can do is cry.

I'm praying to grab a lease on life to help me understand.
Yet every time I grab at love, there's nothing in my hand.
An emptiness comes over me, it's hard for me to explain.
It's filled with the hate and longevity that goes along with pain.

I've always felt I lost something that eluded me so long.
But why can't I find a true love? What am I doing wrong?
Then every time I think I've found true love, it comes too little too late.
I guess that's why I'm all alone and the reason I can't think straight.

FALSE LOVE

Granted it felt so right, my hearts been split in two.
I can't believe you used me. I was so in love with you.
The times we spent together truly meant the world to me.
I thought we had a connection, some kind of chemistry.
Whenever we were together, my heart would skip a beat.
I felt it was destined that you and I should meet.

My heart was surrounded by a wall I thought no one could break.
One kiss from your lips, my pulse took a dip; it was all my heart could take.
I gave you all you asked for. You took it all in stride.
Then I saw the big picture as you took me for a ride.

I can't believe my own stupidity. How dumb could one man get?
Still having you in my life for a while is a time I won't forget.
You never said you love me, you just said, "I like you lot."
I should've read between the lines and ducked the arrow that cupid shot.

I should've walked away from you the first time you told me no.
But my heart was into loving you and I couldn't let you go.
You were like my beckon in the night, an angel so it seems.
I thank the Lord in heaven for allowing me time to touch a dream.

I CAN'T GET OVER YOU

You made me wonder what it's like to really be in love.
I thought we truly had a relationship. You were the hand, I was the glove.
And then you walked away from love, now I don't know what to do.
I'm hurting, my life just ain't the same; I can't get over you.

We shared so many wonderful days, made love all through the night.
We didn't care who was getting hurt even though it wasn't right.
I melted each time you touched me like butter in your hand.
But you would never say I love you this I could not understand.

I couldn't turn my back on you because you meant so much to me.
We had a love like music, we produced a chemistry.
I figured we could just be friends, help one another when we're down.
Someone to talk to when in need, now how crazy does that sound.

I can't blame you for my downfalls, to thy own self be true.
I want to love you forever girl, I can't get over you.
I'm always fighting with these temptations of wanting
to see you more and more.
I just wish the feelings were mutual; I was the one you were yearning for.

Now I'm going to forget the way I feel so these words I write are true.
I'm going to respect your wishes and keep away…
Still I can't get over you.

FOR YOU

Image a world with no worries this is what I would attempt for you.
My everything would revolve around your love and everything you do.
I'm blessed just to have you in my life. You are a part of the chosen few.
I got on my knees and prayed He would lead me to you.

Being with you has opened up new avenues of life.
You're the bow wrapped around the world.
If we were living in the ocean, our origins would be, me oyster, you pearl.
You shine like a beacon in the night; you're my guardian angel on earth.
So I'm taking this time to say, "I love you." You can take it for what it's worth.

I'm not going to summon up more tears. I'm not crying any more for you.
You have managed somehow to hurt my soul when my love for you was true.
I'm covering up my emotions I don't want the world to see.
How loving someone can destroy a man just look what you've done to me.

I was always eager to please you, yes, I opened up my heart.
And you took the love I so freely gave and ripped my soul apart.
Yet for you I attempted to make it work. For you, I took a chance.
I put your love and pain on my shoulders and believed in true romance.

Yet again my emotions were shattered. I started looking at life at a glance.
No more cryin' for you, I've figured out what to do,
I'm going to wait on my love to enhance...
FOR YOU!

LOVING YOU

Loving you is the only thing in life I want to do.
I want to spend every waking moment still in love with you.
It's hard for me to focus on anything else I'm doing.
I'm working on a plan, you understand, your love is what I'm pursuing.

Your smile is like a breath of fresh air. You make me want to sing.
The thought of you excites me. You are my everything.
You own a space inside my heart; you make me want to scream.
Your touch is like magic. In you, I've touched a dream.

Your love is wrapped around me like a protector in the night.
No one could never steer me wrong for loving you is right.
Your touch is like a drug to me. It's hard to understand.
I'm addicted, girl, to loving you. I need a 12-step plan.

I'm in love with loving you. I know this don't make sense.
But when I'm in your arms,
I fear no harm and I know love is about to commence.
Your love relaxes me to a point that I melt like honeydew.
The fact of the matter,
you make my heart pitter-patter because I'm truly loving you.

THROUGH ALL ADVERSITIES

Through all adversities,
I've prevailed and saved myself from the brinks of hell.
I've climbed the ladder to the top then missed a step and down I dropped.
I've hit the bottom so it seems a glitch of sort to spoil my dreams.
My health has hindered my road to wealth, but hell, I did this to myself.
In time, I have noticed the things I've lost.
My health and respect is what it cost.
At times I've imagined my life was through because
I gave all my love to a chosen few.
Yet, love has evaded my world it seems for
I've only touched it in my dreams.
I've coped with relationships in life and it has poisoned
my bein' like a rusty knife.
Love is like an addiction just like drugs and booze,
and like a fruit over ripe my heart has been bruised.
I've givin' up on happiness. I'll never love again.
I'll simply love'em and leave'em, and forever have a friend.
So through all adversities, remember I've prevailed
and when you climb that ladder to the top, remember love is hell.

STUBBORN

There is standing room only in this head of mine
as the thoughts go round and round.
I'm surprised I haven't cracked up or gone crazy 'cause
I jump at the slightest sound.
See my pride has always got in the way of nearly everything I do.
I can't help thinking I'm losing my mind whenever I think of you.

You see, sometimes I dial your number just to hear your voicemail speak.
I'm sure you're the woman I dream about, the love in which I seek.
In my mind I'm developing these pictures of the type of mate I want for me.
The woman I want to share everything I am 'till the end of eternity.

My expectations aren't that high, but I'm stubborn to a point.
Still I'm looking for the love Jesus wants me to have, the one He will anoint.
I'm stubborn in the wildest of ways and my mate should be the same.
I don't want to be just a bump in the road. I don't have time for games.

I'm crazy to have fallen in love with you. I'm stubborn and that's a fact.
But I need you to help me complete my dreams and get me back on track.

Cassius

WHY IS THIS RAGE INSIDE MY HEART?

A calmness fills the empty room as this emptiness invades my heart.
Should I break down and cry, maybe curl up and die,
I don't know where to start.
I've constantly circled around the block just to notice you weren't there.
And then when I finally see your face, I pretend that I don't care.

Like a fool, I thought you could love me until my world just fell apart.
So I ask you in this painful state, "Why is this rage inside my heart?"
There is a war raging inside my loneliness and it's eating away at my soul.
Its job is to completely crush me and it has just about reached its goal.

Tell me, why is this rage inside my heart; tell me why do I feel this way.
It's so hard to do battle with something unseen.
Oh God, make this pain go away.
I keep battling these forces, what is one to do?
Why is this rage inside my heart? Why am I missing you?

There's this pain that exist in my stomach and it's ripping a hole in my chest.
I keep wanting to run, but my will has been stunned,
hurt is living in there like a guest.
I keep telling myself I can handle this,
but the truth is I don't know where to start.
I'll stay in the fight; keep my head held up right,
yet, why is this rage inside my heart?

Cassius

SELDOM SEEN

As the winds blew gently through her hair my eyes fixated on her face.
I couldn't imagine not loving every inch of her body
as she walked into the place.
The color of her eyes amazed me every time I'd stopped and stared.
I'm writing these words in awe of you for your beauty is beyond compare.

The mere thought of you leaves me breathless
no other woman could ever compete.
With the love you give me unselfishly, lady, you knock me off my feet.
You have the body of a goddess and every inch I'd love to kiss.
You're the dream that every man wishes for at the top of his Christmas list.

I figure I was destined to be with you to be the lover in your life.
And hope someday I'll have the courage to say I want you to be my wife.
You strengthen every part of me, I'm the puppet and you're the strings.
I'm filled with joy when I'm with you, you are my everything.

I feel weakened every time I lay next to you, my heart would skip beat.
I'm infatuated by the mere touch of you as we lay between the sheets.
I'm dedicated to living my life with you in my kingdom, you're the queen.
I'm so grateful to be madly in love with you for this kinda
of love is seldom seen.

Cassius

FOREVER FOR ALWAYS FOR LOVE

You will always and forever be in love for the love has made you complete.
It was destiny you two found one another.
He paved the road so you could meet.
He has blessed the two of you with something
that for some take a life time to find.
A love and togetherness that gives you the ability
to know what's on each other's mind.

He blessed you with two children that you cherished from birth 'till grown.
And now they're both loving parents, themselves with children of their own.
Your stability is what dreams are made of. Your love makes a house a home.
Watching the two of you on your anniversary
is what inspired me to write this poem.

I know I'm just the brother of your son-in-law,
you've shown me nothing but love and respect.
And because of that union, this family I was blessed to get.
For forty-three-years you have been together and your union is truly blessed.
I'm sure you two had some bumpy roads and through Him, you passed the test.

The two of you are perfect together; you fit like a hand in a glove.
It's obvious you'll always be together
FOREVER, FOR ALWAYS, FOR LOVE.
Cassius

LOVING SOMEONE MEANS SOMETIMES SAYING GOODBYE

I'm trying to ignore these feelings and no matter how hard I try.
It's true that loving someone means sometimes saying goodbye.
It may not be what you want to do and the timing may not be right.
You knew from the start she was breaking your
heart so are the feelings you try to fight.

It's obvious this shouldn't be and you know you're living a lie.
It's true that loving someone means sometimes saying goodbye.
They're not worthy of the love you give, yet you give it anyway.
And now you're finding it hard and complicated to pull yourself away.

You see them every other day and it hurts your heart so much.
But the only thing that's on your mind is her love, her feel, her touch.
You're pushing your heart to the limits and your hair is turning grey.
You try to forget about loving her but these feelings won't go away.

You have pictures of her etched inside your mind
and like a slideshow you review.
The images of loving her hurts so bad it's slowly killing you.
Loneliness has engulfed you, sadness fills your soul.
Erasing the images in your mind has become a lifetime goal.

Still every time you delete one picture another one appears.
The thought of her fills the wells of your eyes and you compensate with tears.
You cry so much your eyes are puffy; they look like you've been in a fight.
But you can't erase the way you feel so you cry throughout the night.
You're searching your soul for an answer;
the pain is so intense you want to die.
Just remember it's true that loving someone
sometimes means saying goodbye.
Cassius

PRECIOUS LOVE

You were the lightning bolt that struck me, the arrow in my heart.
Now you're the reason I'm stuck in loneliness, oh yes, you played a part.
You had my heart within our grasp. You turned me upside down.
I can't believe I'm thinking long and hard about keeping you around.

I'm gradually gathering strength again though at times I may need a shove.
To keep me from running back to you for you are my precious love.
I sit back in my solitude and see images in my mind.
Then I wonder is there somewhere on this earth true love will I ever find.

Sometimes at night when I curl up with my pillow,
I can still smell your perfume.
Then I squeeze my pillow tighter because my heart is filled with gloom.
Your love is like an addiction just one taste and I was hooked.
Not worried one bit about the consequences and the chances that I took.

I truly thought you were the one for me sent from the heavens above.
I thought for sure I had found my equal. I had found my precious love.

Cassius

SAY YOU LOVE ME

I've convinced myself I'm vulnerable and this is right where I should be.
The day I looked deeply into your eyes and asked you to say you love me.
I've been praying someday the time would come
and I wanted it to be with you.
From the moment we met this whole moment's been
set and now I know not what to do.

I've been carelessly searching for a love that someday I could call my own.
But I would never go surfing the internet or try to find love on the phone.
I'm going to search until I find you, no matter where you are, I'll be.
And there I will stand with my outstretched
hands waiting to hear you say you love me.
I will continue to look until I find the
one who makes my world complete.
It's in Jesus' hands for He's laid out the plan,
only He knows when we shall meet.

Cassius

GROW OLD WITH YOU

I loved you the first time I saw your face. I knew it was meant to be.
You're the angel I've been praying for. God lead you right to me.
From the moment I held you in my arms and kissed your lovely face.
I knew then you were the one for me, no one could take your place.
I need you to complete me, to change my wrongs to right.
To guide me from the darkness and lead me to the light.
They say all good things come to those, but I don't have time to wait.
I yearn to have you near me, no time to contemplate.
My soul is slowly calling, slowly calling out your name.
Yet, each time I say it in my mind, I'd replay it and it never sounds the same.
You have given me the will to live and you don't even know me yet.
I would do anything for you, if not, I would regret.
Not doing what you asked of me, would render me no soul.
To have you in my life would mean my dream will now unfold.
I am telling you my secret thoughts 'cause I need for you to know.
My body burns in loving you for my heart it tells me so.
I want to spend every waking moment making all your dreams come true.
Please give me the opportunity. Please let me grow old with you.

Cassius

TO REACH THE UNREACHABLE

With my outstretched hand,
I'm focused on grabbing something that's not really there.
It's unfortunate I can't control this journey, but who said life would be fair.
My nerves are on edge, I'm in misery as I face the inevitable.
And I have to face the fact that it is impossible to reach the unreachable.
My life is in disarray as I contemplate ending this pain I feel.
But taking one's life is not Christian like and I'm trying to do God's will.
I'm in mourning for my own life. I feel like my soul has passed away.
I cry out to Jesus for spiritual guidance, each night on my knees I pray.
I'm so tired of fabricating a world in my mind that is free from worry and pain.
I feel like I'm going insane.
It's hard to deal with the fact I'm searching for something
I know is untouchable.
I'm trying my best not to be like the rest
and I'd someday reach the unreachable.

Cassius

GAMES

Love is not a board game where you move from space to space.
Love is an emotion felt by two and I surely take the case.
I fall in love like a drunk does down the stairs.
Flat on my face in loneliness, but no one seems to care.

I've had some ups and downs in my life. It's clearly plain to see.
But all my downfalls have a blame and that blame falls right on me.
I've tried to buy a lover that was clearly a mistake.
And every time I tried that route, it was all give and take.

I'd give everything I had and they took it all away.
I grew accustom to this 'cause it always went this way.
I'm getting used to living alone and being by myself.
One thing's for sure, there is no cure and I may just find some wealth.
I hope someday to find love. I wonder what it's like.
To find someone to share my dreams and be two on a double bike.

Yet every time I think I've found someone, it winds up just the same.
I'm caught up in this maze of pain, yet it's all part of the game.

Cassius

SOMEDAY YOU'LL KNOW

I've never done anything to hurt you, but I let my feelings show.
It was a love that was not supposed to be so I had to let you go.
Someday you'll know that letting you go was hard for me to do.
'Cause now that you're no longer in my life, I'm really missing you.

Although you're hundreds of miles away, I still see your lovely face.
I can almost smell your sweet perfume and your lips I yearn to taste.
Someday you'll know just how I felt the day I knew we couldn't be.
It's as if you dug deep into my chest and snatched the breath up out of me.

But I'm slowly getting over you and I'm sure someday I will.
And someday you'll know how much it hurts; you'll see just how I feel.
No I'm not wishing nothing bad on you for I love you still today.
Someday you'll know the difference and this pain will go away.

Cassius

I KNOW WHAT I DID WAS WRONG

I dipped into a forbidden fruit where I knew I shouldn't be.
But the attraction was kind of animal like, you can say it took over me.
My judgment may have been coerced a bit still I knew what I was doing.
I was out of my mind. I should have followed the signs,
but your love I was pursuing.
I couldn't commit myself to you 'cause we knew it wasn't right.
Still I couldn't help it the thought of you still I fought with all my might.
Sometimes I wrongfully accused you of things you didn't do.
That's when it became painfully obvious I was falling in love with you.

It's forbidden sometimes I would tell myself as I held you close to me.
But it felt so right to be wrong and I asked, "Don't you agree?"
It was hard for me to deal with the truth I wasn't the only man holding you.
Yet, I stood in line like all the other guys, part of the chosen few.

And now because of my past transgressions, I find myself alone.
I can't blame anybody but myself, I created this on my own.
I should've never opened Pandora's Box's;
this union was doomed from the start.
Now the only thing I have to show for
my pain is my constantly hurting heart.

I knew what I was doing was wrong. I can't make no sense of it.
Seems I'm facing a life of darkness and the path has just been lit.

Cassius

REPLACING YOU

I'm having a problem in my life and I don't know what to do.
This dilemma I'm having is killing me, the thought of replacing you.
I'm lonelier now then I've ever been.
You have no idea what I'm going through.
How did I ever get in this predicament, the thought of replacing you.

I'm crying inside, I can't handle this. It's all happening all too fast.
My life is now covered with gloomy dark clouds. I walk around under an over
cast.
As the raindrops fall from the clouds over head and mixes in with my tears.
My eyes are now open to the fact that I must learn to face my fears.

The light at the end of the tunnel called life is now turning from white to blue.
I'm still hurting inside but the tears have
not dried from the thought of replacing you.
As the moment of truth is approaching, a decision must be made.
I'm not ever going to get over you it's like holding a live grenade.

Sooner or later, I'm going to have to pull the pin as this storm begins to brew.
Let's face it you're part of what completes my being. I'm never replacing you.

Cassius

I'M DOING JUST FINE

I have fallen like a leaf from a tree, slowly falling to the ground.
I haven't quite landed on my feet still my life is spiraling down.
The mere thought of losing everything is so fresh inside my mind.
Yet, through all adversities I'm doing just fine.

I'm struggling; yes, I'm fighting just to make my endings meet.
But I'm humble and content at times to land on my feet.
I'm trying not to show weakness and I'm looking for a sign.
I'm focused on not showing hurt so to me, I'm doing just fine.

My thoughts are like a bird in flight, soaring gracefully through the wind.
I'm going through a crisis now and I don't know where it ends.
I'm finally at peace with my past and now focused on what's ahead.
But I still have these images of the wrong
I've done still swimming in my head.

I opened up my heart for help and the wheels began to grind.
And while those wheels of life are against me now, I'm doing just fine.
While the closet door of life keeps closing and I want to draw the line.
It's time to face up to the problems in life so I'm truly doing just fine.

Cassius

CLEARED THOUGHTS

SILENT RAGE

Children dying.
Silent rage.
Mothers crying silently.
Who's trying to educate?
Too late, a child's fate.
Silent rage.
As the chamber engages, you hear a sound.
Another round.
A child's body hits the ground.
Silent rage.
We see school violence across the country.
Drugs, gangs and guns.
Is this the silent rage we seek?
Has our longevity reached its peak?
What peace do we seek as another child dies?
Silent rage.
We scream for safety in schools.
Are parents fools?
Are our homes safe?
Is this where it starts?
Are we not a part of the dying society?
The young getting slayed by the gun.
Although they say, "It don't exist."
I still get pissed.
At racism, I shake my fist.
Each time a black youth pulls a trigger,
To a racist, just another dead nigger.
Hearts being broken.

Forums being spoken.
Holding back theses tears,
I choke in silent rage.
I stand alone as the wells of my eyes fill.
The death rate of our children increases throughout the years.
Silent rage.
We attempt to teach peace.
But like the crease of a pair of jeans the streets are mean.
Our teaching's is what I call seldom seen.
I sit and I watch my watch as time ticks by.
I ask myself, "Why, why, why, why do they die?"
Silent rage.
Two young men open fire on a school,
This ain't cool.
Lives taken.
My Savior's words forsaken.
More risk must be taken to instill the way.
I feel it's God's will.
I will instill peace in our children.
Put an end to the sins.
Silent rage, silent rage, silent rage.
Is this truly our last days?
Is the revelation upon us?
Who do we trust?
Is there anyone amongst us?
Yes, I must confess.
Jesus is amongst us, again.
He died for our sins where silent rage begins.
Oh, ye of little faith, has the Devil casted a bid for your souls?
Sins untold.
Lives unfold.
The end is cold.
Yet, bold is He who sits in the mist of the almighty.
Who will again put an end to the sins?

Silent rage, silent rage, silent rage.
How do we compete or stand what is the plan?
When the laws protect the Klan.
You understand I'm but one man.
Yet, in my hands I hold my truth.
Christ is the proof as the world goes *POOF*!
Silent rage.
Even Christ is in rage.
Silent rage.
Now, set the stage.
We're all just pawns in the game of life.
Be it husband, be it wife.
It's your life, it's your life, it's your life.
Silent rage.
Tell me, why do we fly across the seas?
Are these people truly our enemies?
Bush and Chaney are getting rich on stock.
Our young men and women are dying in Iraq.
Silent rage.
I seek peace.
When will violence cease?
Why can't love increase?
Or will we continue to cry?
Watch our children die.
Parents get high.
Yet, we still ask, "Why, why, why?"
Silent rage, silent rage, silent rage.

OUT OF THE TUNNEL & INTO THE LIGHT

As the clouds gather in my head and the darkness shades the light.
My emotions become conceded as I fight it with all my might.
My subconscious mind has gone back in time
and my subliminal mind has gone blank.
I felt mentally blinded, labeled criminally minded;
into the darkness of this hole I sank.
No matter how hard I concentrate I can't focus, it's out of my site.
I'm fighting like hell, I have no one to tell; I start crying out into the night.

Now I search for self-gratification to bring happiness back into my life.
Yet, I have no support, I'm fighting in court and I'm losing the love of my wife.
I'm not worthy of the love I was getting from her and deserve everything I get.
I reach out for her hand, yet alone I still stand, hurting her I now truly regret.

I'm trying to get out of this hole I've dug and I know I'm in for a fight.
I'm struggling and doing everything I can to get
out of the tunnel and into the light.

A WASHED-UP GARBAGE CAN

They walk this world amongst us; it could be woman, it could be man.
A person faking an image is nothing but a washed-up garbage can.
They say the things you want to hear just to see what they can get.
In the long run, you'll find, excuse my language, they were full of shit.

Politicians are masters of this field, out of their mouths the lies flow faster.
But the most devious one in this field of shit
is the one some choose to call pastor.
I'm not trying to say all God's disciples are bad but there
are some that walk this land.
Just to fill their pockets from the collection plates, a washed-up garbage can.

Their focus in life is to rob you of your wealth and dreams you're holding.
They're nothing but cheats and lairs or as they say, a fox in sheep clothing.
A family member, a so-called friend, the one wearing the wedding band.
Don't be fooled, let your faith be the tool to spot a washed-up garbage can.

STRUGGLING

I've gathered all my past dreams and have come to the conclusion; dreams are moments in time put together in scenes, collectively portraying life, yet in the wake of it all, the dark images have taken on a life of its own
which we choose to call struggling.

Which in hindsight, is the body telling the mind to adapt and overcome, though sometimes over looked, pain is an emotion, a quite powerful emotion if used correctly can be used to battle the emotional killer we choose to call struggling.

Struggling; ends not meeting, kids not eating.
Struggling; car not running, pockets no money.
Struggling; war on the tellie, no food in your belly.

Life in its own existence is a struggle, our ancestors were the pioneers of struggling, what we call struggling today, they called freedom, we tend to take advantage of the word choice, we pretend it don't exist and tunnel vision ourselves into a world of failure which we choose to call struggling.

We place blame on everyone and everything, yet as we blame, we are the ones reaping the rewards of a condemned life instead of embracing a challenge, we build boundaries to try and defer the challenge which then metamorphose into a problem which we choose to call struggling.

There is purpose in each of us, we were all born with the gift of choice, Jesus died, our ancestors died, King died to secure that, yet some still choose to sit in the mist of darkness, a darkness called self-inflicted failure
which we choose to call struggling.

LIFE CHANGE'S (ALONE)

I've come full circle. I've begun where I began.
Life's changes have engulfed me, my daytime has no sun.

Alone I have encouraged my selflessness to rise above life's changes, but I've
come full circle. I've begun where I began.
Life's changes have engulfed me, my daytime has no sun.

Time has seemed to stall each night. I have the same dream; there is never a
curtain call. I have fallen into the obis of loneliness, yet still I've come full
circle. I've begun where I began.
Life's changes have engulfed me, my daytime has no sun.

Repeating this vicious cycle has hurt me to the core, yet still I'm grateful
every morning my feet touch the floor. Like a battered leaf in the wind, I float
gracefully outside, my being noticing I've come full circle.
I've begun where I began.
Life's changes have engulfed me, my daytime has no sun.

I crave to reach a destiny. I seek to touch a dream. The harder I strive for
greatness, the further away it seems. My mind sees my accomplishments. I
celebrate within, yet I've come full circle. I've begun where I began.
Life's changes have engulfed me, my daytime has no sun.

My thoughts are still frames, a slideshow for all to see. Have I shamed the
only part of me that is not a mockery? Self-centeredness has corroded the
relationship I had with myself. I now face life's changes alone because I've
come full circle. I've begun where I began.
Life's changes have engulfed me, my daytime has no sun.

QUITE ANGER

I feel like a political refugee caught up in a presidential race.
And because of my military affiliation, certain dangers I now face.
Mortars crash all around me as my blood begins to boil.
In my mind I hear, "Bush should have his ass over
here dodging mortars for fucking oil."
My quite anger seems to peak each time I hear his lying voice.
It's easy for Bush to send more troops because
as the president that's his choice.
Yet quite anger engulfs me as I think of all those who died.
Those young men and women over in Iraq all because some recruiter lied.
Still politicians are getting rich, their little plot I'd love to foil.
And stop the senseless killing of our children overseas on foreign soil.
Quite anger is seen on the faces of parents. I see the anger when they speak.
Why are they there, does our government care, an answer is all they seek.
Now that a holy war is upon us, we know not who to trust.
Politicians are lying, more parents are crying; American blood in Iraq dust.
Iraq, Iran, Afghanistan at war within itself.
But our leaders are the ones reaping the spoils and gaining all the wealth.
It's amazing how quickly wars begin and the reasons for which we fight.
But what makes Bush think he's the savior
that can change their wrongs to right.
We have homeless and drug trafficking,
injured veterans struggling to make ends meet.
At the rate we are going,
the pain will keep pouring and we're bound to taste defeat.
As an injured veteran it angers me that we can spend billions to fight a war.
Yet, I sit here injured with my case for benefits pending;
what the hell are we fighting for?

ALREADY THE FORGOTTEN

An injury not only physical but mental just as well.
Will one get over these adversities? Only time will tell.
Some are in pain every day, yet we fight pain just like the war.
We focus in on survival and what the next day has in store.

Didn't this war on terrorist start because of Osama bin Laden?
I thought we caught Saddam but just like Osama,
some vets are already the forgotten.
They give us awards and certificates but what good will this paper do.
The things the vets went through after Vietnam I now see it was true.

The push through the system goes very quick to get you to Iraq.
But where's the honor in fighting for freedom
when the government turns its back.
What is the true purpose behind this war?
What the hell is George Bush plottin'?
KBR is making millions on the death of our children,
something in the White House sure smells rotten.

Is it Bush? Is it Chaney? Is it Condoleezza Rice?
Is it terrorism or is it oil? Is it freedom for a price?
Over two-thousand and something casualties, and it shows no sign of stoppin'.
Yet those at home decapitated and injured are already the forgotten.

THEY'RE ALREADY HERE

Homeland security, what a joke, let me make this perfectly clear.
The terrorist they're trying so hard to keep out, believe me,
they're already here.
We hear about the terrorist cells in the country just waiting to react.
I'm sure they're in our communities preparing for another attack.

They have billions of dollars at their disposal and access to our basic needs.
They have properties all around the world and to them, they hold the deeds.
We know how they use the cell phones. As they say, "When it rains, it pours."
Who's to say they're not rigging the cell phones
we are buying from their stores.

Understand we buy our meat from these people.
They have access to the foods we eat.
I'm not trying to bring chaos to the problem at hand
but some could be dying as we speak.
My thoughts and opinions are mine alone and for my country, I do fear.
I'm clearly stating these cells are waiting. I'm afraid they're already here.

We're over there fighting as Bush says, "To preserve their way of life."
That pain you feel in your back is the war
and George Bush is wielding the knife.
So clear your thoughts of 9/11 and be aware of what to fear.
Let the government worry about those trying to get in
and watch those that are already here.

QUESTIONS

An event in which you can't understand; a process that began with the mind;
not being able to grasp the moment.

We question war because we can't see the logic in the death of our children.
We question our government with 9/11 and Katrina,
and the gulf coast is still struggling to rebuild.
Yet Chaney and KBR are reaping the rewards
of the death of Americans in Iraq.
We question the statements of the Mayor of New Orleans.
How much more time must he waste?
Would the help come any faster or is the mayor just a bastard trying to cover
his mistakes with race.
We question the whereabouts of Osama since Saddam has already been caught.
But our troops are still fighting and dying,
and Osama bin Laden is still being sought.
We question our homeland security level and why isn't it always high.
They don't elevate until it's way too late or they blow a plane out of the sky.
We question veterans benefits 'cause so many still struggles to cope.
Some have become unemployed with no hope to fill the void,
some veterans turn to dope.
We question the questions because if we don't question,
the questions we'll still have.

TO HURT IS HEALING

As painful as reality is with pain there is relief.
In suffering there is strength to help you deal with grief.
Emotions are a part of life. It enhances the way one's feeling,
Some just can't understand God's master plan and to hurt is healing.

If you gather up all the adversities you faced since first you spoke.
Life is going to throw you some bumps in the road.
Don't treat them like a joke.
Death is inevitable. It's just when that we don't know.
To hurt is healing like your tears they're revealing the emotions
you fail to show.

We imbibe our existence, yet do things to expedite our being.
We do things without thinking like drugging and drinking.
It seems from life we're fleeing.
Can you cancel out your feelings? Can you fight the way you feel?
To hurt is healing, no pain is revealing, we are all of flesh, not steel.

FREE—DUMB

Freedom, F.R.E.E.D.O.M. is what our ancestors fought and died to get.
Free-dumb, F.R.E.E.D.U.M.B. is what our children are living with.
Some have no clue of what they went through or how many lives were given.
Some were beaten and hanged, some endured hunger
and pain for the world in which we live in.
Our ethnic race has been challenged. We're facing slavery once again.
But not at the hands of prejudice whites, but our own black on black sins.
We stopped educating our children on how we got to where we are.
They are too interested in video games and who can build the hottest car.
You don't see educational stories any more.
We stopped sitting them down to teach.
Our roots, Dr. King, Malcolm X, we need to practice before we preach.
If we spent more time on our children, we wouldn't have to scream.
My ancestors died for you to be free, we're the ones killing the dream.
We celebrate Black History Month in February which
is the shortest month of the year.
Showing commercials on television has nothing to do with why we're here.
I'm not saying they're not educational and a purpose in life they do play.
But those few second they show on television won't make history go away.
Let's be aware of our children's teachings and be involved in which they come.
Teach our children to be proud of who
they are and don't just be free and dumb.

THROUGH THE EYES OF A CHILD

I can only imagine how you must feel or how hard your life must be.
I can only sense the pain you feel from what I hear and see.
I know there is anger inside of you. It's enough to drive you wild.
But I can't see life as you see it, through the eyes of a child

Like me, I know you want to be loved; structure is what you're searching for.
You have to give respect to get respect. It's like a revolving door.
I see some lash out at others. I try so hard to understand.
I want to take away their pains, just lend a helping hand.

I want to say there's something better, wipe their tears and watch them smile.
I wonder what thoughts are in their minds, through the eyes of a child.
Some are in a bad situation and their parents gave in to the streets.
These children are just as strong as your average adult;
living day to day is an amazing feat.
They endure all of life's tribulations, bumpy roads and trials.
And we can never truly comprehend their pain 'till we see
through the eyes of a child.

BECAUSE OF THEM

Every time I remember why I can sit at the front of the bus.
I can't help but think of the ancestors who gave their lives for us.
Martin Luther King wanted peace, Malcolm X wanted to fight.
Yet both of them are not here today, but we have our civil rights.

Rosa Parks would not give up her sit, Harriett walked the rails.
Now we can't stop killing each other and most are locked up in jails.
Young black men are being raised by the streets,
young women are just the same.
Crack has endangered a whole generation and it's hindering their rise to fame.

Are athletes are being stereotyped because of all the money they make.
Still they take most of the money back when said athlete makes a mistake.
Our ancestors fought and died for our freedom
and we're slapping them in the face.
If we continue to keep killing off our young, we won't even have a race.

The black man is already fighting extinction because of drugs,
alcohol and guns.
With Bush still making these major cuts, the government won't have no funds.
Like a batter we have to step up to the plate
'cause our existence is looking slim.
We're on the brink of losing all they achieved.
What we have is because of them.

SOME DON'T KNOW. DID YOU?

Some don't know our heritage or how we came to be. What we so aimlessly take advantage of, the right to say, "I'm free." Did you?

Some don't know in the 1700 and1800s, the government passed a law that allowed trappers to go from state to state and recapture free slaves. Did you?

Some don't know in 1846, a self-educated slave named Samuel Burris, who was a free slave, was recaptured and returned to the Deep South and resold. Did you?

Some don't know a white Quaker named Flint, who was an abolitionist worked with two others named Stills and Garrett to outbid other traders for the rights to own Mr. Burris. Did you?

Some don't know after Mr. Flint out bided the other traders he watched as Mr. Burris stood afraid and crying. Mr. Flint walked passed the other traders, stood next to Mr. Burris, leaned over and whispered in his ear, "You're a free man, again. You were just bought with abolitions gold." Did you?

Some don't know Miss Tubman made over nineteen trips into the Deep South via underground railroads to assist the efforts of runaway slaves. Did you?

Some don't know during those dangerous journeys, another white man, Thomas Garrett assisted her by giving money, food, clothes, shoes and hope. Did you?

Some don't know during that time a black man condemned to a life of slavery wanted freedom so bad that he shipped himself to freedom in a wooden box. His name is Henry "The Box" Brown. Did you?

Some don't know some white people didn't approve of the Declaration of

Independence because it didn't include African Americans. Did you?

Some don't know a vast majority of African Americans don't know a damn thing about the true struggles to be free or the countless white people who assisted. The help given by white abolitionist, *all we know* is we struggled to be free, but we haven't done a thing. We haven't struggled, our ancestors, the Tubman's, the Burris's the Brown's, Malcolm X, Mr. and Mrs. King, Mrs. Rosa Parks and also the Garrett's, the Flint's; these people risked their lives, the lives of their families for us to live free. Did you?

King and Malcolm sacrificed their lives for freedom, a dream and so far the dream has become a nightmare. We as a race are slowly killing ourselves. We sell drugs to our own people! Did you?

We're destroying ourselves, be it Black, White, Hispanic, Jew, Christian, the dream is we all could live together and respect each other as an equal. Did you?

Another famous white man said, and I quote, "A house divided against itself cannot stand." This was Abraham Lincoln. Some didn't know hate is not genetic, it's taught and that's pathetic. Did you?

PARDON ME, IT WAS HIM

A corrupt police department, a system based on lies.
Innocent men incarcerated, now Americans, here their cries.
See black men were arrested, tortured and beat.
In the South, cops rode horses, wore white hooded sheets.
A white witness and a lineup was clearly all it took.
A telephone book, a few left and right hooks and the police produced a crook.

They beat me, they punched me; look at the bruises on my face.
Two white officers and a black man, and this has nothing to do with race?
We've been crying out for freedom for years, what justice did this bring?
They're filling up prisons like slaves ships. I thank God for Dr. King.
D.N.A. is the future of law enforcement
and now the innocent are being acquitted.
But back in the day, they flipped the D and the A.
It meant, Another Nigger Did It.

Now inmates are crying out for redemption about
the crimes they didn't commit.
Like Johnnie C said in the OJ case, "This damn glove doesn't fit!"
Then as soon as election time starts growing
near and the margin of victory is slim.
That's when the Politian's start hearing those inmates,
who scream, "Pardon me, it was him!"

CONFRONTED

Aren't we at some point the blame for the tragedies that hit?
Don't you feel that in certain places, we put our nose were it doesn't fit?
Iraq, Iran, Saddam, Vietnam, I pose this question,
"At what point did these countries pose a threat to the U.S?"
Look at the facts, aren't we still paying large amounts for oil and gas.
I say we are confronted with the fact we're fighting to preserve the relationship
we have with big oil tycoons,
who in turn take our money to buy our gas stations, liquor stores and 7-11s.
In fact, we are putting our life sources in the hands of potential terrorist.
Aren't we confronted now with the fact
we are now being forced to be racially bias.
Terrorism isn't genetic. It's taught. Now, I'm not saying all Muslims are
terrorist; but yet, unbeknownst to me, the same guy
I'm buying meat from could be a terrorist.
A doctor, a soldier; are we not confronted with enough inner American turmoil
without having to concern ourselves with third world countries?
Yet now we are confronted with our own backyard being the thrust of terrorist
attacks. Our government's actions are now being judged.
I myself don't approve of the war but as an American, I support our troops.
We are confronted with the fact these people are smart, not only did they use
our planes to attack us, they used our kindness, our training, our technology,
our box cutters, our mail system, our people.
Tell me how does one expect to launch a surprise attack when before you do it,
you broadcast it on national TV?
We have sent thousands of our young men and women to fight in wars
to restore their way of life when we have yet to confront
the problems we have right here at home.
Are we now confronted with the fact our government is sending our young
people untrained to a foreign soil to die. Yet here at home,
we still have homeless, hungry, dying, American
problems that have not been confronted.

WE ALL DESERVE TO LIVE

We've given so much of ourselves for freedom this is true.
But is our government holding back on the benefits by law they owe to you.
Vietnam, Desert Storm, Operation Iraq Freedom; are we now fighting for oil?
Are we the dumb ones for leavening our safe abode to go fight on foreign soil?
Although I didn't know what I was fighting for, no one asked me if I cared.
But I've done some things that now cause bad dreams; can't forget I was there.

Now I'm reaching out to my government for the help they should freely give.
I'm an injured vet, yet what respect do I get? We all deserve to live.
Bush said war was relevant and we're fighting for freedom, right.
But he's not the one sweating under the sun and fighting insurgents every night.
There were young men and women lying
on the ground with blood on their shirts.
I listened to one take his last breath, now for me just breathing hurts.
There are times when I feel I've done something wrong
for the service I choose to give.
I wasn't forced to sign it but by contract I'm binded,
still we all deserve to live.

PAST TENSE

The future, the days ahead of you that's not promised day-to-day.
Kirby Pluckett was just 44-years-old and just recently passed away.
It seems we're leaving here earlier these days.
They say the dirt will come out in the rinse.
Now you're stressing about where you are with God
and your past has made you tense.
You're looking at all the aspects of your life;
what you're doing is straddling the fence.
You seem egger to jump,
in your throat there's a clump and your life seems cold and dense.
You start developing habits that hinder you more than help.
Now you're waiting for life to commence.
The things you've done have you now on the run
and your decisions just don't make sense.
See, you're fighting a battle inside yourself and have been fighting it ever since.
You started stressing about the things you use to do,
letting your past make you tense.

IN YOU, I SEE ME

Like the image of one's self, in a mirror my reflection tells a story.
A time in my life I'm not proud of, it was shameful, painful and gory.
I need something powerful to cling to. There are steps to recovery you see.
Your part of my plan, I hope you understand without you,
there would be no me.
I want to keep you in my equation, we have a good chemistry.
Still you must understand you placed my life in my hands
so I'm doing this just for me.

I will need your support on this journey. It's a quest I must complete.
I've been drug'n so long and my cravings are strong,
but I won't give in to defeat.
Now don't take these words out of proportion,
you're a part of my master plan.
It's clear I can look at all the chances I took.
Now I need you to hold my hand.
With you in my life, I can make it; my recovery does not come free.
For your strength is my crutch and I need you so much,
don't you know I see you in me.

THE ROAD I TRAVELED

I'm carrying around a lot of frustration and it's starting to wear me down.
But believing in Jesus has eased it some, in Him some peace I've found.
I'm hurting so much these days because my life has become unraveled.
Due mainly to the bad choices I've made and because of the road I've traveled.

It was inevitable in my life that I would soon come to this point.
My body hurts all over. I feel pains in every joint.
I've begun to make U turns in life and the path I took was graveled.
Yet, I've always managed to find my way back to the road I traveled.

I picked up habits on my journey, some good and some were bad.
I can't change the choices I made and sometimes that makes me sad.
I've confused my family and friends. I've done things to leave them baffled.
But I've changed my ways from this road I've paved,
I now cherish the road I traveled.

I WANT TO LIVE

I've given so much to this country, too much sometimes it seems.
For me, I've given up the ability to even have sleeping dreams.
Some are coming back disabled and not knowing what to do.
Confused about war and what we were fighting for,
some people turned their backs on you.

At night my head is so clouded with images it's hard for me to sleep.
It's the images of war that makes me dive to the floor,
into my dreams these images creep.
My thoughts run rapid in my head; sometimes the pain is so intense.
It's like standing in a puddle of water and holding on to an electrical fence.
I sit in my house with thoughts of dying because I am so bored.
Now I fight off these thoughts with all my might, I've seen the crazy wards.
My mind is so jumbled with memories. I'm trying hard not to give in.
If I don't get a hold of this problem, the demons are going to win.
So I'm sitting here taking a look at life and I have so much I can give.
I won't give in to the dreams I'm having because I want to live.

BACK WHERE I STARTED

I'm never going to let myself down again that phase in my life
I have now departed.
I'm not going to go down that dark road again.
If I do, I'll be back where I started.
I'm beginning to find peace in my life again. I have found an inner space.
What was once just an isolated part of my being is now replaced with grace.
I have come too far to start over again and lose everything I've earned.
But through all these trials and tribulations, there's a lesson to be learned.

I'm now fighting to keep pace with the world
and not get lost in my sickness again.
I know doing the things I was doing in the eyes of the Lord is still a sin.
I'm content to grow stronger every day in His world, I'm sure I will.
But it's up to me to find stability when unloved is how I feel.

See mere words can't express all the pain I've felt.
I was known as the broken hearted.
And if I can't find a way to disguise this anger,
I'll be right back where I started.
There is a moral to these words I'm writing, but it eludes me yet again.
If back where I started is where I am destined to be, then this is where I'll end.

INTERNAL DUMPING GROUND

I often isolated myself. I jumped at every sound.
I couldn't hold a conversation when people were around.
Resentment always clouded my thoughts. I was always feeling down.
My world was engulfed in sadness, an internal dumping ground.

My feelings were so jumbled up; my mind was in a haze.
I walked around in darkness. I looked like I was dazed.
I couldn't control my emotions on my face. I wore a frown.
Still people just kept throwing shit at me, an internal dumping ground.

I couldn't hold my head up; my fear was running deep.
They were even throwing shit at me when I laid me down to sleep.
I often thought of moving, of finding peace in another town.
What's the logic in that, in every town there's crack,
an internal dumping ground.
I have to dig myself out of this sickness no matter what drugs are around.
I'm no longer a clown; in Christ's strength I have found,
I'm no longer an internal dumping ground.

FOCUS & CONTROL

So simple one's life can be, the secret I've been told.
The common denominator to living straight is focus and control.
My focus was so unclear to me until a new friend steered me right.
I was focusing on things I couldn't control. I was blinded by the light.
I couldn't see the answers, yet they were right before my eyes.
I couldn't control my addiction. I was living a life of lies.
My focus was on the negative things happening in my life.
I was too controlling and always angry that's why I lost my wife.
My self-control was lingering; my world was falling apart.
My focus was not on living. I was damaging my heart.
Now today I'm focused on the positive and controlling the things I can.
I have focus and control, gave Jesus my soul and my life is in His hands.

WHATEVER IT TAKES

Whatever it takes to get over this I've decided I would do.
I've punished my body long enough, now it's time to get rid of you.
You've beaten me up for far too many years, now it's time I let you go.
You have coned me and lied, you're the thorn in my side;
you've been killing me very slow.
I've been living with you for over 25 year. Let me go for goodness sake.
I know I can't hide in the world you preside, but I'll do whatever it takes.
To make you stay away from me, I'll do everything I can.
I won't let you take me down again. My life is in my hands.
There is a God. He's with me now to help me in this fight.
I'm going to defeat theses demons that haunt me in the night.
How do you kill a demon just like you kill a snake?
You cut his head off, watch his body go soft, you do whatever it takes.

MOTHER, I MISS YOU

I hurt inside my heart for you. I cry out loud at night.
I'm trying to get my life together I'm trying to do what's right.
I've stumbled in certain spots and I found this to be true.
There's this emptiness inside of me. , I miss you.

I'm missing the conversations we had. You were there every time I'd call.
And every time I made a mistake in life, you picked me up each time I'd fall.
You instilled in me your loving ways, see, I respect everyone I meet.
To my elders, I always used sir and maim whenever I would greet.

I'm always trying to better myself because you told me I should.
You taught me the importance of raising the bar to get out of the hood.
Your wisdom is running through my veins like water through a stream.
Still mother I miss you so much. I search for you in my dreams.

I truly could use your guidance for I feel so lonely now.
I wish you were here to dry each tear I cry when no one's around.
I have a mental picture etched inside my mind for whenever I'm feeling blue.
But it will never replace your loving face. Mother, I'm missing you.

FROM THE BOTTOM TO THE TOP

I've often asked the question, "What has happened in my life?"
Through my addiction I've lost everything I had,
my money, my home, my wife.
As thoughts of drugs run through my mind, my body starts to chill.
Due to my isolation and past frustrations, cold and lonely is how I feel.

I've cried out to my higher power to help me in this fight.
He answered, "My son, you have choices you choose.
You know the difference between wrong and right."
My life was crumbling around me as I sat in my house in shame.
I was sticking my use on my family when it was me who was the blame.

As teardrops feel down to the floor, I searched deep inside my soul.
I saw my life for what it's worth and the end was bleak and cold.
I brought on all this misery. I'm suffering because of me.
I'm in this dark predicament because I choose to be.

Bad dreams of war are haunting me at night. I toss and sweat.
I cry out because of some of the things I've done, some things I now regret.
The act of taking another man's life is with me every day.
I keep telling myself it was me or them but the dreams won't go away.

Has my family turned its back on me after all I've done for them?
Or am I just pointing the finger at them because my life is looking grim?
I can't believe what I've done to me and why this came to be.
But I looked at myself in the mirror today and I'm likening what I see.

I was having thoughts of suicide, but my higher power made them stop.
To Him I would pray, now I can safely say,
I have dug my way from the bottom to the top.

THE END

I've crossed the threshold of my addiction and now I've closed the door.
But on the other side where my cravings hide, I don't know what's in store.
I'm searching for a new horizon; it's time to test my will.
I'm still emotionally unstable. I am not the man of steel.

Oh my recovery will be challenged and I'm still a loaded gun.
Can I face life on life's terms or should I just break and run?
My self-esteem has cancelled out my depression. I can face myself again.
My pain has ended, I'm no longer offended, I have serenity within.

I called on my higher power and searched honestly through Him.
My world has been brightened with Him.
I'm now fighting; my world is no longer dim.
I punished myself long enough. I look back on life and grin.
I've been waiting so long for this moment where I can finally say...

THE END!

CPSIA information can be obtained at www.ICGtesting.com
Printed in the USA
LVOW10s0723040916

502792LV00001B/6/P

9 781612 444116